CAMBRIDGE LIBRARY COLLECTION

Books of enduring scholarly value

Travel and Exploration

The history of travel writing dates back to the Bible, Caesar, the Vikings and the Crusaders, and its many themes include war, trade, science and recreation. Explorers from Columbus to Cook charted lands not previously visited by Western travellers, and were followed by merchants, missionaries, and colonists, who wrote accounts of their experiences. The development of steam power in the nineteenth century provided opportunities for increasing numbers of 'ordinary' people to travel further, more economically, and more safely, and resulted in great enthusiasm for travel writing among the reading public. Works included in this series range from first-hand descriptions of previously unrecorded places, to literary accounts of the strange habits of foreigners, to examples of the burgeoning numbers of guidebooks produced to satisfy the needs of a new kind of traveller - the tourist.

An American in Iceland

Samuel Kneeland (1821–88), educated at Harvard and in Paris as a doctor, served as an army surgeon during the American Civil War. After the war, he returned to lecturing on physiology, and expanded his academic interests to zoology and to natural history in general. His expedition to Iceland was fuelled by a fascination with volcanoes, volcanic islands and the flora and fauna that abounded on them, but Kneeland was as much a cultural and historical tourist as a scientist, enjoying the millennial celebration of the first settlement by Norwegians, the spectacle of geyser eruptions, and the Norse history and traditions of the Icelanders. This 1876 work offers a chronological account of his party's travels through the Scottish islands and around Iceland, bringing a very individual touch to a description of the country, its culture and its outstanding landscapes.

T0381934

Cambridge University Press has long been a pioneer in the reissuing of out-of-print titles from its own backlist, producing digital reprints of books that are still sought after by scholars and students but could not be reprinted economically using traditional technology. The Cambridge Library Collection extends this activity to a wider range of books which are still of importance to researchers and professionals, either for the source material they contain, or as landmarks in the history of their academic discipline.

Drawing from the world-renowned collections in the Cambridge University Library and other partner libraries, and guided by the advice of experts in each subject area, Cambridge University Press is using state-of-the-art scanning machines in its own Printing House to capture the content of each book selected for inclusion. The files are processed to give a consistently clear, crisp image, and the books finished to the high quality standard for which the Press is recognised around the world. The latest print-on-demand technology ensures that the books will remain available indefinitely, and that orders for single or multiple copies can quickly be supplied.

The Cambridge Library Collection brings back to life books of enduring scholarly value (including out-of-copyright works originally issued by other publishers) across a wide range of disciplines in the humanities and social sciences and in science and technology.

An American in Iceland

*An Account of its Scenery, People,
and History, With a Description of its
Millennial Celebration in August 1874;
With Notes on on the Orkney, Shetland and
Faroe Islands, and the Great Eruption of 1875*

SAMUEL KNEELAND

CAMBRIDGE
UNIVERSITY PRESS

CAMBRIDGE UNIVERSITY PRESS

Cambridge, New York, Melbourne, Madrid, Cape Town,
Singapore, São Paolo, Delhi, Mexico City

Published in the United States of America by Cambridge University Press, New York

www.cambridge.org
Information on this title: www.cambridge.org/9781108049726

© in this compilation Cambridge University Press 2012

This edition first published 1876
This digitally printed version 2012

ISBN 978-1-108-04972-6 Paperback

BAYARD TAYLOR.

C. W. FIELD.

DR. KNEELAND.

M. HALSTEAD.

DR. HAYES.

AN

AMERICAN IN ICELAND.

*AN ACCOUNT OF ITS SCENERY, PEOPLE,
AND HISTORY.*

WITH

A DESCRIPTION OF ITS MILLENNIAL CELEBRATION
IN AUGUST, 1874;

WITH

NOTES ON THE ORKNEY, SHETLAND, AND FAROE ISLANDS,
AND THE GREAT ERUPTION OF 1875.

BY

SAMUEL KNEELAND, A.M., M.D.,

SECRETARY AND PROFESSOR OF ZOÖLOGY AND PHYSIOLOGY IN THE MASSACHU-
SETTS INSTITUTE OF TECHNOLOGY.

With Map and Nineteen Illustrations.

BOSTON:

LOCKWOOD, BROOKS, AND COMPANY.

1876.

Cambridge:
Press of John Wilson & Son.

TO

HON. JOHN AMORY LOWELL,

Trustee of the Lowell Institute,

THESE PAGES, IN THE MAIN PREPARED AS INSTITUTE LECTURES,

ON HIS KIND INVITATION, ARE RESPECTFULLY

DEDICATED BY

THE AUTHOR.

PREFACE.

I HAD the satisfaction during the summer of 1874 of visiting Iceland, on the occasion of its celebration of the thousandth anniversary of its settlement by Norwegian rovers. I was led to this distant, and supposed cold and cheerless, region by several motives, prominent among which were : 1. The desire of comparing its volcanic phenomena, exhibiting the singular paradox of extensive glaciers and eruptions of fiery lava and boiling geysers in close proximity, with those of the Sandwich Islands, which I had visited in 1872. Having gazed into the horrible cauldron of the "Lake of Fire;" having witnessed the magnificent spectacle of Mauna Loa and Mauna Kea, fourteen thousand feet high ; having toiled to the top of Haleakala, ten thousand feet, and stood within its extinct crater, twenty-seven miles in circumference, — I longed to see Mount Hecla, which conceals under its mantle of perpetual snow volcanic fires which have many times spread desolation for several miles around its base. 2. The hope of collecting specimens of natural history from this isolated region; and 3. The desire of seeing its curious and remarkable people, enjoying the rare celebration of the thousandth birthday of their country.

We are making extensive preparations to celebrate the one-hundredth anniversary of our national independence in 1876; and we naturally call to mind the great advance of our country and of the world in that century — political, educational, financial, social, and religious — in which America has taken a most prominent and honorable part. But what has Iceland done for humanity or for itself, that it should publish to the nations its millennial celebration? It has done much for liberty, the advance of knowledge, and the preservation of historic records; and at a time when other more favored nations were stationary or going back to the darkness of ignorance and superstition, — and under conditions of isolation and hardship, which prove that man is superior to his surroundings, and that misery cannot stifle the aspirations of liberty, nor degrade a poetic and heroic race.

I propose to take up the subjects in the following order: —

1. What we saw on the way, including the islands to the north of Scotland, all at some time invaded or inhabited by the same race that peopled Iceland;

the reader is thus better prepared for the Icelandic national traits, and will better understand their history, especially its relation to maritime discovery and the settlement of Greenland and America five centuries before the time of Columbus.

2. The royal reception in Iceland, and the commencement of the festivities, with an account of the strange physical conformation of the island.

3. The volcanic phenomena of Iceland with the millennial celebration in the lava valley of Thingvalla.

4. The Geysers and Mount Hecla.

5. The characteristics of the people.

6. Their history, present condition, and hopes in the future.

In addition to my own experience, I have consulted all original works on Iceland within my reach, from Banks and Van Troil in 1772 and 1780, Olafsen and Paulsen, Mackenzie and Henderson, to Professor Anderson's writings in 1875. Information received since the text was stereotyped has been embodied in "Notes" at the end of the work. The reader is referred to these in advance, especially the latest account from a friend in Iceland of the great eruption of 1875.

The illustrations have been made by the "Photo-Engraving Company" of New York; the greater part of them from original photographs obtained by me in Iceland.

Though in many cases incorrect, I have adopted the spelling of Icelandic names most familiar to English readers, lest I should be suspected of affecting a knowledge of the Icelandic language which I do not possess. In many cases I have used the phonetic spelling, as better than the native assemblage of consonants and vowels, which, if not unpronounceable, seem often unnecessary. I think the interest of the book will thus in no wise be diminished.

S. K.

Boston, Oct. 20, 1875.

LIST OF ILLUSTRATIONS.

———◆———

CONTENTS.

———◆———

CHAPTER I.

THE ORKNEY ISLANDS.

CHAPTER II.

THE SHETLAND ISLANDS.

CHAPTER III.

THE FAROE ISLANDS.

CHAPTER IV.

OFF FOR ICELAND.

CHAPTER V.

CELEBRATION AT REYKJAVIK.

CHAPTER VI.

PHYSICAL CHARACTERS OF ICELAND.

CHAPTER VII.

THE VALLEY OF THINGVALLA.

CHAPTER VIII.

THE CELEBRATION AT THINGVALLA.

CHAPTER IX.

ROUTE TO THE GEYSERS.

CHAPTER X.

IN THE VALLEY OF THE GEYSERS.

CHAPTER XI.

THE OLD NORSEMEN.

CHAPTER XII.

THE PEOPLE OF ICELAND.

CHAPTER XIII.

POLITICAL HISTORY OF ICELAND.

CHAPTER XIV.

DISCOVERY OF AMERICA.

CHAPTER XV.

LITERATURE OF ICELAND.

CHAPTER XVI.

VOLCANIC HISTORY OF ICELAND.

CHAPTER XVII.

GEOLOGY AND MINERALOGY.

CHAPTER XVIII.

ICELANDERS IN AMERICA.

CHAPTER XIX.

THE FUTURE OF ICELAND.

CHAPTER XX.

USEFUL INFORMATION.

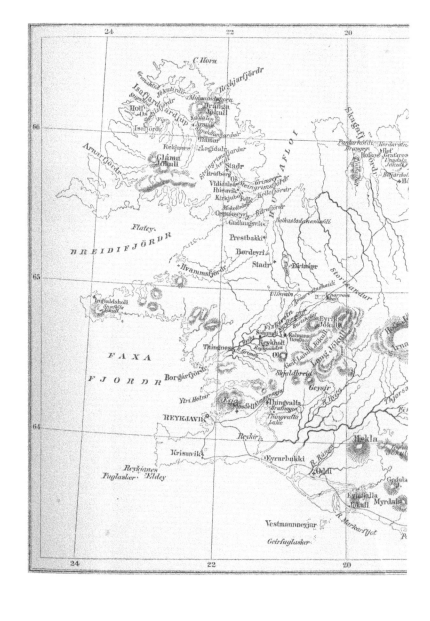

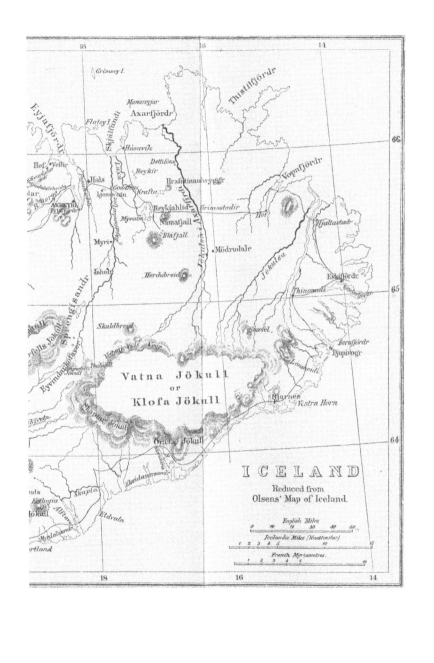

ICELAND

Reduced from
Olsens' Map of Iceland.

English Miles

Icelandic Miles (Hrathnilar)

French Myriametres.

AN AMERICAN IN ICELAND.

CHAPTER I.

THE ORKNEY ISLANDS.

> " But I remember when we sailed
> From out that dreary Forth,
> And in the dull of morning hailed
> The headlands of the North :
> The hills of Caithness, wrapped in rain ;
> The reach of Stroma's isle ;
> The Pentland, where the furious main
> Roars white for many a mile, —
> Until we steered by Shapinsay,
> And moored our bark in Kirkwall Bay."

THE considerations mentioned in the preface impelled me to recross the Atlantic ; encounter
the rough seas, chilly fogs, and dangerous navigation
of the Northern Ocean ; and submit to the cold rains,
scanty food, miserable shelter, and toilsome travelling
which I had reason, from travellers' tales, to expect in
Iceland.

1*

Our party consisted originally of five Americans: Mr. C. W. Field, of Atlantic cable fame; Dr. Hayes, the Arctic explorer; Bayard Taylor, the traveller-poet; Mr. Halstead, of the " Cincinnati Commercial ; " while I represented New England and some of her scientific and educational institutions. Not being a correspondent of any newspaper, and having no business interests to serve, I went solely to see the country and become acquainted with the characteristics of the people. When we met in the north of Scotland, we were joined by a younger son of Mr. Gladstone, ex-Premier of England, and by a native Icelander, Mr. Eric Magnusson, sub-librarian at Cambridge University, England, and professor of the Scandinavian languages in that university, who was invited to go with us, and who rendered us invaluable services, both in our intercourse with the people and the authorities, and in making the necessary arrangements for our trip into the interior, to witness the millennial festivities.

We fitted up, manned, and provisioned a small but staunch screw steamer of about 200 tons, the "Albion," at Edinburgh. She was commanded by Captain A. Howling, of Leith, a fine specimen of the British seaman, whose ideas had been enlarged by acquaintance with other countries than his own, and to whose knowledge of the northern islands and of Icelandic waters much of our enjoyment from a sense of security was due. Owing to some ridiculous provisions of the English laws, we found it necessary, in order to get away through maritime legal meshes, to enrol ourselves in the shipping-office as British sailors for the voyage, promising to uphold the honor and dignity of Great Britain, and to behave ourselves like good seamen. After signing the papers in due form, we sailed from Leith, the port of Edinburgh, on the 20th of July, 1874; or rather I sailed, the rest of the party joining the steamer at Aberdeen, whence we sailed on the 22d for the Orkney Islands. English-speaking travellers should approach Iceland, as we did, by way of Scotland, the Orkneys, Shetlands, and Faroe Islands. All these bear traces, both in language and customs, of the old Scandinavians, the Norse vikings, sea-kings, — or pirates, if you will, — who settled in these islands and in the north of Scotland before the historic period. The volcanic character of the scenery, which attains such a remarkable wildness in Iceland, begins even in Edinburgh and its surroundings to attract attention. All this region of the Northern Ocean, even to Jan Meyen, has been the scene of terrible volcanic disturbance, and bears marks not only of fire, but of the irresistible glacier and of the tremendous blows of the Northern Ocean. The transition from " Arthur's Seat " to Mount Hecla and the chasms of Thingvalla is geologically a very natural one.

Our party met at the Douglas Hotel in Aberdeen, after a deal of trouble. Arriving, as we did, some from Edinburgh, some from London, and others from the North of Scotland, each sought his room at night or early morning. Like many other Scottish hotels, this one kept no register, and therefore it was impossible to ascertain the names of those who arrived; and being, from short acquaintance, unable to give such a description of each other as "boots" would understand, we were in blissful ignorance of each other's proximity, until hunger, which fortunately pervades the human economy every morning, brought us together in the breakfast-room.

We wandered about the clean and picturesque city, reminding me much of some of the business-parts of Boston in its granite-faced buildings and stores. Making a few purchases of water-proof clothing, I soon found that the Aberdonian sharpness in trade, against which I had been warned, was such that one could easily believe the story that an unfortunate Jew, who undertook to do business there, was soon starved out. Talk about shrewdness: the Yankee is very far inferior to his Scotch cousin.

We started about 6 P.M. in a drizzling rain, a small wharf-committee being in attendance, attracted by the unusual sight of a steamer bearing both the American and the English flags, and one, so small, about to visit the distant and dangerous shores of Iceland. We were obliged to wait until the high tide would allow the docks to be opened. The sea was calm, except a long swell, and gave no indication of the "Spanish waves" we encountered in the Northern Ocean. The rain soon ceased, and the sunset-clouds were very beautiful in their ever-changing hues and their reflections on the water. Soon after coming in sight of the spires of Peterhead, a fog set in, forcing us to go very slowly through the returning fleet of fishing-boats, which answered our shrill warning-whistle with a melancholy, pitiful toot. We arrived in the harbor of Kirkwall, the capital of the Orkneys, the next morning about nine o'clock, dropping anchor quite near the shore.

The Orkneys — distant only fourteen hours by steamer from Aberdeen, Scotland — are very beautiful as seen rising from the blue waters of the summer Northern Sea; some are low, others high; some with quiet beaches, others with wave-washed cliffs. The fields are green, the birds numerous on land and water, and the air has that peculiar exhilarating character, of mixed sea and land breeze, which is noticed at such places as Nahant, Nantucket, the Isles of Shoals, and Mount Desert. Even in Edinburgh, the

American is astonished to find that he can read in the open air at nine in the evening. This length of day grows more and more conspicuous as you go north toward the midnight sun. In the Orkneys, the sun rises in summer at about 3 A.M., and sets about 9.30 P.M.; the longest day being 21 ½ hours; the shortest being from 9 A.M. to 3.15 P.M., or 6¼ hours, in winter. The daylight seems to linger almost to midnight, and the coming daylight of the morrow seems to arise, almost without interruption, from the light of the preceding evening.

This is neither the time nor place to detail the bold and cruel deeds of the northern sea-kings. Their early history is involved in obscurity; but we know that these islands were certainly settled about 400 B.C. by Picts, — by some considered a Teutonic, by others a Celtic race. Here their barbarous hordes lived till they were overpowered by the Roman emperor Claudius, A.D. 53. These islands were known to the Roman historians as the Orcades. Three centuries afterward they were conquered by the Saxons. All these northern nations worshipped Odin, till the introduction of what was then considered Christianity, in the tenth century. Christianity — as forced by King Olaf of Norway on the Jarl Sigurd, the principal chief of the Orkneys — consisted simply in the administration of baptism, without any attempt to explain its doctrines; and the so-called conversions of that time, and unfortunately many other conversions in other lands in more modern times, comprehended nothing more than the performance of a ceremony meaningless to those who adopted the name of the new religion. When Norway was subdued by King Harald Haarfager, in the middle of the ninth century, many of the petty chiefs with their followers went over to the Orkneys and the islands to the north, where they established themselves, plundering the mother country when opportunity offered. This so exasperated the king that he sent an army to conquer them, placing over them rulers, or jarls, of his own selection. These in their turn invaded Scotland, whose northern parts show many traces, both in people and ruins, of the Norse element. After centuries of fighting with each other, invading England, Ireland, and Scotland, they embraced, as has been stated, Christianity, in the tenth century.

Among the most interesting things in Kirkwall is the Cathedral of St. Magnus, begun in 1137 by jarl Ronald, in memory of his uncle, basely murdered by his cousin Hacon twenty-seven years before; this he built in conformity with a vow, made in case of victory over the Scotch, that he would erect in Kirkwall a church whose magnificence should be the wonder and admiration of future ages. Magnus Sec-

ond succeeded to the jarldom in 1231, and from him
Alexander, king of Scotland, took Sutherlandshire,
which up to this time belonged to the jarldom of
Orkney. William, son of the Earl Henry who died
in 1420, was the last of the Orkney jarls. Alexander
III. of Scotland had agreed to pay Norway 100 marks
yearly for the cession of the Western Islands. No
payments having been made from 1426 to 1457, Norway became impatient for the £10,000,000. Charles
VII. of France, as arbitrator, recommended a marriage between the Prince of Scotland and the Prin-
cess of Denmark. This was effected in 1468, Orkney
being given as security for the payment of 50,000
florins, and Shetland was pledged for 8,000. The
islands were never reclaimed, and were annexed in
this way to the British empire in that year, under
James III., and have since been in the hands of several families, and are now in the Dundas family.

Kirkwall, the capital, is a place of great antiquity,
with a good harbor and considerable shipping. The
streets are narrow, often steep, and well paved; the
houses are very quaint-looking, and a Sunday stillness seemed everywhere to reign, the greater part
of the idle male population having gone down to the
quay to see the (to them) almost unknown American
flag. Their curiosity was not intrusive, and they directed us with eager politeness.

The great point of interest here to all travellers, the Cathedral of St. Magnus, is more than seven centuries old, quite perfect, and one of the best specimens of the early Gothic architecture in existence. It is very surprising to see in this out-of-the-way place, of a few thousand inhabitants, a massive church of red sandstone, 226 feet long and 56 wide, the cross or transept being 92 by 28; 71 feet high inside, and 140 to the top of the present spire. Its colonnades, arches, doors, and windows are worthy of examination by all lovers of architecture. The cross is the oldest part, containing four massive Gothic pillars, 24 ft. in circumference, spanned by five arches, the central spire resting upon these; and the six pillars next are perhaps even older. In the choir is the famous Gothic "rose-window," three and a half centuries old, 36 feet high and 12 feet wide, of four arches, separated by three stone divisions, surmounted by the twelve-leaved rose. The three bells, of almost equal age, are rung by the feet and hands, the tongues being made to strike against the side of the bell. The west or principal door, three centuries old, still shows traces of its elaborate stone carvings. The interior is simple and grand, somewhat marred by a portion walled up to the roof to accommodate in comfort the more tender congregations of the present time. The aisles and floors contain several strangely

B

sculptured stones, marking the resting-place of many Norse celebrities. The steeple looks stunted, having been almost destroyed by lightning in 1671, and never rebuilt. From the top is a magnificent view of the town and many of the adjacent islands and ruined buildings.

Among the noteworthy ruins are those of the Bishop's and the Earl's Palaces. In the former, of unknown but great antiquity, King Haco of Norway died in 1263; the tower now standing was built by Bishop Reid in 1540; it is circular on the outside, but square on the inside, containing on the outer wall a statue of himself; the staircase is so decayed that the ascent is now forbidden. The Earl's Palace, near the cathedral, is also in ruins, a monument of the cruelty and oppression of the famous Earl Patrick Stewart, who in the sixteenth century defied the power of the king, laughed at laws, robbed and murdered the people, compelling them to build his castles and palaces in several of these islands; the same tyrant oppressed the people of the Shetlands, till his crimes became so intolerable that he was seized, and carried to Edinburgh, where he was beheaded in 1615.

Our party then took a carriage to the Mound of Maeshowe, about nine miles from Kirkwall, one of the most important antiquarian discoveries in Great Britain. It is a large mound of earth, of circular

shape, 36 feet high, and 90 feet in diameter, surrounded by a shallow trench 40 feet wide. It contains a central chamber 15 feet square and 13 feet
high, from which branch off three cells, to the north,
south, and east, about 3 feet high, and from 5½ to
7 feet long, and 4½ wide; the roofs, floors, and back
walls are each composed of a single stone, and each
could be closed by a single stone, found on the floor.
On the west side is the door-way, 2⅓ feet high and
wide, giving access to a passage 54 feet long, of large
stone slabs set on edge, opening into the chamber.
Probably it was originally a great chambered barrow
on the surface of the ground, afterward covered with
stones and earth from the surrounding trench. Antiquarians are not agreed as to the age of this mound,
but the most probable opinion is, that it was built as
a place of burial for distinguished personages by the
Celts or Picts, as early as the eighth or ninth century. Though the architecture is primitive, the work
must have required much time and labor. It had
evidently been opened at some remote period by the
Norsemen, as the stones in the interior were found
scattered about, with much rubbish. The walls are
covered with runes and inscriptions of various dates,
most of them belonging to the Norwegian division
of the Scandinavian class, and not older than the
middle of the twelfth century. There are more than

one thousand inscriptions, and many figures of animals, one of them a winged dragon, pierced by a sword.

On the road to Maeshowe is a miserable-looking hamlet, of about two hundred souls, called Finstown, interesting for nothing but the fact that its few inhabitants require for their spiritual needs three churches, — the Established, Free, and Independent: the second having the finest building. This was to me the most pitiful exhibition of theologic bigotry and narrow-mindedness that I had ever seen. I was not unacquainted with the puerile divisions of like character in some of our New England towns, where each "ist" or "arian" sect must have not only its own preacher, but its teacher, doctor, grocer, blacksmith, and haberdasher of the same theologic stripe; never meeting in friendly intercourse or interchange of opinions, but each travelling stiffly in its narrow rut, which it fondly believes is the sole path of salvation; each hugging its grain of truth as if it were the whole truth, — but Finstown is entitled to the prize for the "least possible amount of Christian charity." When will these bitter sectarians discover that theology is not religion; that creeds are not truths; that blind faith, selfish pursuit of present or promised happiness, and obedience to the letter, regardless of the spirit, of supposed divine law, are not virtues!

Why will they not cherish the spark of eternal fire which they have in their hearts, without attempting to smother that which burns as brightly in the bosom of their neighbor of another belief! why declare their tiny rill from the fountain of the Father's love the only pure one, and all others from the same source "waters of perdition!"

Within a few minutes' ride of Maeshowe are the remarkable stone circles of Stenness, in groups or solitary, standing like sentinels over numerous grass-covered mounds of various sizes and shapes. These stones seem at one time to have formed two or parts of two circles; in the series near Maeshowe, only three stones are left, — two standing, and one on the ground; the last is 18 feet long, 5⅓ wide, and 21 inches thick, and had apparently been inserted 2 feet in the ground. A similar pillar stood near by, having a hole cut through it about 5 feet from the ground, which doubtless served as the altar to which the victims for sacrifice were fastened ; but in more modern times lovers met at this " Stone of Odin," and pledges made when their hands were joined through this hole were considered as sacred vows. It is not standing now. Walter Scott, in his novel, " The Pirate," has introduced this stone as a trysting-place. If this promise by the stone of Odin was sacred for lovers, the neighboring church of Stenness was equally convenient for those weary of married life; if the couple, after entering the church, separated, and one went out at the north door, and the other at the south, they were legally divorced, and free to make another visit to the " stone with a hole in it."

On the other side of the loch is the great circle of Brogar, a circular platform of stones, about 13 feet from the margin of which, and in a diameter of 340 feet, are the "standing stones,"—thirteen upright, and ten on the ground; originally there were about sixty stones, 17 feet apart; the average height is 10 feet, and width 5½; though smaller than the first-named circle, they are sufficiently large to strike one with astonishment how such blocks could be hewn and placed in position with the mechanical devices then known. Their purpose was probably of a religious character. They were doubtless of Celtic Druid origin, and not erected by the Northmen. The numerous grave-like hillocks mark the place of a great battle fought by two Norse jarls about the year 960.

A few miles west is the town of Stromness, well known to geologists by the discoveries of fossil ganoid fishes, made there by Hugh Miller, and familiar to Boston readers in his work, " Footprints of the Creator, or the Asterolepis of Stromness," containing facts bearing upon the theory of development, inasmuch as these oldest vertebrates known were of a very high type among fishes. In his own words, the old red sandstone of the Orkneys "furnished more fossil fishes than every other geological system in England, Scotland, and Wales, from the coal measures to the chalk, inclusive. It is, in short, the 'land of fish,' and could supply with ichthyolites, by the ton or ship-load, the museums of the world."

Stromness, famous for its rushing tides and spacious land-locked harbor, though historically modern, is geologically of immense antiquity; it is on the margin of a beautiful bay, in whose waters in the Devonian age sported the huge sharks and ganoid fishes so graphically described in Miller's works. Though the town is poorly built, it has a very picturesque look, many of the gabled houses running to the water's edge, and having their own separate piers.

The "Wizard of the North" has thrown his charm around this place. Captain Cleveland, in Scott's "Pirate," was John Gow, son of a merchant of Stromness; he was commander of the "Revenge," of twenty-four guns, and frequently visited the harbor and gave dancing-parties there, before his real character was known; he was captured by stratagem, in 1725, in one of the sounds of the neighboring island of Eday, and soon after executed in London.

An old hag, named Bessie Millie, who sold favor-

able winds to the fishermen, lived here, and was the
original of his strange character of " Norna of the
Fitful Head."

The " Torquil " of Lord Byron's " Island," was
George Stewart, whose father resided in Stromness.

The scenery in the vicinity of Kirkwall is very
tame ; the roads are excellent, flanked on each side
by stone walls surmounted by slabs set on end, like
a conglomeration of narrow tombstones. There were
a few fine houses, surrounded by well-cultivated fields
and a general prosperity was indicated by abundant
crops of hay and sleek cattle. The roofs of the
poorer houses were thatched with straw, kept in
place by flat stones fastened by ropes of straw, for
the same purpose doubtless as the stones on the top
of the Swiss *châlets*, to keep them from being torn
off by the violence of the winds. There were extensive fields of oats, barley, and potatoes, in which
the sun-browned women were working with the
men.

The islands are 67 in number, of which 27 are
inhabited, and 13 of considerable size ; they contain
nearly 400,000 acres, of which about one-fourth are
cultivated ; the population is about 32,000, supported
by agriculture, fishing, and the manufacture of hosiery
and formerly of straw plait. Pomona, or Mainland,
on which the capital is situated, contains about half

the population. The highest elevation is 1560 feet, in the island of Hoy. Peat-bogs abound in the islands, but the winds prevent the growth of trees ; the temperature ranges from 25° F. to 75°, the mean annual heat being 45°.

Life in these islands is uneventful, there being no excitement except that arising from the perils of the sea ; we saw no signs of beggary or extreme poverty ; our horses' hoofs startled strange echoes as in a deserted village ; but the signs of the post-office, telegraph-office, and Bank of England showed that even this remote region was alive to the events and business of the parent country. The Norse element was evident here, and contrasted with the Norman-French characteristics of the southern Channel Islands ; the Celts, doubtless, occupied the northern islands for a long period before the Northmen.

2

CHAPTER II.

THE SHETLAND ISLANDS.

Rock Scenery. — Rough Seas. — Fair Isle. — Sumburgh Head.
— Early History. — Lerwick, the Capital. — Scalloway
Castle. — Tingwall. — Peat-Cutters. — Scott's "Pirate."
— Bressay Cave. — The Holm of Noss. — Sea-Birds. —
Anderson Institute and Asylum. — People. — Hosiery and
Shawls. — Shetland Ponies. — Departure for the Faroes.

" North, ever north ! we sailed by night,
And yet the sky was red with light,
And purple rolled the deep.
When morning came, we saw the tide
Break thund'ring on the rugged side
Of Sumburgh's awful steep ;
And, weary of the wave, at last
In Bressay Sound our anchor cast."

THE Shetland Islands, the next natural stopping-
place on the way to Iceland, are more high
and picturesque than the Orkneys, and their rock
scenery on the verge of the ocean is unsurpassed,
as far as I know ; every variety of rock form, from
the colossal pyramid to the magnificent arch and
immense cavern, all fashioned by the fury of the
wind and waves, may here be seen ; beautiful in clear
weather, they are frightful in the storm and fog, the

rush of the waters and the screams of the disturbed sea-birds betokening peril to the mariner; we were there in rough weather, but with the power of steam we could defy the surrounding dangers, which have proved fatal to many a proud sailing vessel, from the time of the Spanish Armada to the present day.

We sailed for Bressay Sound and Lerwick at five P.M., having taken a pilot to guide us through the rather dangerous channel into the open sea, which a strong headwind had lashed into waves which made our little steamer roll and plunge in a way that soon revealed to most of the party that their sea-legs had not yet been acquired; she had behaved so well in the voyage to Kirkwall that we began to think the Northern Ocean was not so rough a place as voyagers made it out; but it now seemed as if some marine tarantula had bitten her, and she began to dance in a most lively and persistent manner. The old saying is, "send a man to sea, if you wish to know what is in him;" and we soon found out our individual value as measured by Neptune's rude standard.

Midway between Orkney and Shetland is Fair Isle, a mass of rocky precipices inhabited by about three hundred fishermen, and surrounded by such tempestuous seas that no boats can leave or enter its two unsheltered harbors sometimes for several weeks. In 1868, during a fog, a German emigrant vessel, "The

Lessing," from Bremen for New York, was wrecked between two of its high cliffs; there was no escape above, but all of the many hundred passengers were saved through a subterranean gallery in the rocks. It is a cruel misnomer to call this useless rock, and dangerous impediment in a foggy and stormy ocean, by the name of Fair Isle. In rare, calm weather, it may seem fair to the summer voyager; but for the greater part of the year it is a terribly fatal snare. Many a noble vessel, freighted with precious lives, has been dashed to pieces on its rugged cliffs. It would be a blessing if by some convulsion, similar to the one which raised it from the deep, it could be again engulfed. It is quite unfit for human habitation, as its occupants now seem to be convinced.

The southern points of the Shetlands, especially the high cliffs of Sumburgh Head, are exceedingly picturesque, — the sea dashing upon them with great fury, and one can call up in imagination pictures of the shipwrecks which must have occurred here. We reached this promontory about midnight, but, soon after seeing the light, a thick fog shut down upon us, and we went slowly and noisily along, to avoid the numerous herring fishers, whose tanned sails looked like black wings in the obscurity. The fog lasted till after sunrise, so that we seemed to be in mid-ocean, though land was not far off all around us.

The early history of the Shetlands is about the same as that of the Orkneys, the same northern Picts having settled there more than three hundred years before Christ; Tacitus mentions the Orkneys as having been discovered by Agricola, and that Thule was seen from them; so that the Thule of Tacitus is no doubt the island of Foula, the westernmost of the Shetlands. About 910 A.D., Harald subdued these islands, and placed in command over them the famous Jarl Sigurd, the founder of the race of powerful vikings who ruled the northern seas for six hundred years, invading Scotland and other parts of Great Britain, and savagely fighting among themselves. One of these, Einar, was called Torf-Einar, and deserves to be mentioned always with gratitude, as he was the first to induce the people to use turf for fuel, the cutting and preparing of which is now one of the most important industries of the islands. Christianity was forced upon these islands by king Olaf of Norway, at the same time as on the Orkneys, about the year 1000, A.D.

These islands contain a population of about 32,000, and the capital is Lerwick, near the middle of Mainland, the largest island of the group, with over 4,000 inhabitants; the houses are huddled together, on the

steep hill-sides, and remind you of a great arsenal; it
is believed to be the worst-arranged town in the kingdom for the convenience of getting about, accommodating only those who wish to discharge cargoes, or
smuggle goods directly at their doors from a boat
underneath. It will be sufficient to say that the
town owes its existence to the Dutch fishing trade
of the seventeenth century, to explain its peculiarities; at one time (1653) there have been in its fine
harbor ninety-four English men-of-war, and in old
times fifteen hundred Dutch fishing vessels. The
principal industries of the place are for the men fishing, and for the women the making of the famous
Shetland shawls and hosiery, and the cutting and
preparation of turf for fuel, — a delicate and a dirty
occupation combined, as you often see a barefooted
Shetland knitter at work bearing on her back a pannier
of fuel for the market.

About eight miles from Lerwick is the village of
Scalloway, with its old picturesque ruined castle, built
in 1600 by the forced contributions from the people
by the notorious Patrick Stewart, beheaded for his
crimes, as before stated, in 1615. It must have been
an elaborate structure in its day, with its round tow-
ers, whose traces are still evident; the people are eloquent on the wickedness of its builder, and show the
traveller an iron ring in the wall from which many

of his victims were hung, and a small apartment in the thick walls where he hid himself from his pursuers, being finally discovered by the smoke of his pipe.

Scalloway bay is a fine harbor, and the place was for a long time the capital of the islands. In passing through Tingwall, on the road to Scalloway, we are strongly reminded of the Norse names and customs; Tingwall is the same as the Iceland Thingvalla, the "place of meeting of the Council;" and on an island are seen the remains of one of their courts of justice, where the people occupied seats along the shore, in the open air, the judge and his officers being seated in the centre of the island. Here they dispensed stern and swift justice, tempered by mercy, which might follow an appeal to the assembled multitude.

Our ride to Scalloway and back was rather a dismal one; the sky was overcast, the hill-tops were hidden in a thick mist, which the wind sent down upon us, chilling and wetting us almost like rain; the roads were muddy and hilly; the wetness of the grass forbade the collection of many flowers growing along the road-side; the valleys and the hills were disfigured by the strippings and pits of the peat gatherers; the houses were few and miserable; strings of wretched-looking women, barefooted and bareheaded, passed us, bending under the loaded baskets on their backs; even girls of twelve years of age were seen, beginning their young lives as beasts of burden, round shoulders, curved spines, and sad faces telling of the labor which deformed both body and mind. The sunshine would have enlivened the scene; but, as it was, the singularity of the spectacle lost much of its interest by its physical and human dark shadows.

As we returned, we came near peat-pits six or eight feet thick, running up the hills and down into the valleys, of great richness. On an inland sheet of water we saw an old Pictish castle, of thin stones, surrounded by a stone wall; this was open at the top, about forty feet in diameter, and thirty feet high, with walls so thick as to allow a passage-way within them. No mortar was used in its construction, the long, thin, flat stones being accurately fitted together. It reminded me, in some respects, of the round tower of Newport, R.I.

In summer there is almost a perfect day here, a golden gleam being left by the setting sun; and the twilight is so brilliant that at Lerwick in June one can read by it at midnight.

Many of the localities on this island have been rendered memorable by Walter Scott in the "Pirate," and especially Sumburgh and the Fitful Head, and Jarlshof, and one almost fancies he sees the wrecked

Cleveland, Mertoun, and Norna about these rugged precipices. But beyond all these scenes in time, come before him visions of the old Norsemen, the marks of whose occupation are everywhere around him, and whose bold and bloody deeds invest all these northern islands with a singular interest, becoming stronger as he approaches Iceland, whence they started on their piratical expeditions.

As specimens of the scenery of the Shetlands, may be mentioned two places on the island of Bressay, just opposite Lerwick and a few miles to the east, and in full view; viz., the cave of Bressay and the Holm of Noss.

The entrance to the cave is under a wide and lofty archway, worn by the winds, waves, and frosts, the isolated pillar of which is called the " Giant's Leg ;" entering the cavern, the walls of which are of varied and brilliant colors, near its entrance, is a smaller cave, in which a sailor, pursued by the press-gang, secreted himself ; neglecting to secure his boat, which drifted away in a storm, he was a prisoner there for two days, at the end of which time he swam to the outside rocks, and managed to climb to the top of the cliff, several hundred feet high. The large cavern makes a sudden turn, and its darkness requires torches, by whose light can be seen a lofty and large hall, beautifully ornamented by stalactites and pillars,

2* c

from the decomposition of the rocks and the infiltration of water holding lime in solution.

Just to the east of this island is Noss, or the Holm of Noss, an isolated mass of rock, 200 feet × 160, and 160 feet high, rising on all sides almost perpendicularly from the sea. The distance across from Bressay is about 100 feet, though it looks like a very narrow crevice from below. The tops of the island and the holm are nearly level, and covered with a coarse grass, in which the herring gulls build their nests, almost covering it with their eggs. Before 1600 no one had scaled this rock, but in that year an expert climber gained the summit, a line was thrown across, and soon two stout ropes were stretched from the island to the holm, and a communication by means of a sliding box or cradle was established. The sides of the cliffs are also lined with innumerable birds, whose various colors add beauty to the scene, to which their screams and the roar of the waves add a strange and startling music.

A traveller in this region was once tempted to fire a gun at a cormorant. "What became of it," said he, "I know not. The air was darkened by the birds roused from their repose. Thousands hastened out of the chasm with a frightful noise, and spread themselves in troops over the ocean. The puffins came wondering from their holes, and regarded the universal confusion with comic gestures ; the kittiwakes remained composedly in their nests (below), while the cormorants tumbled headlong into the sea. But the confusion was soon over, and all returned to their former places and employments."

Fearing the occurrence of accidents this cradle conveyance has now been removed, and the birds can once more breed in peace.

Nowhere are these grand rock masses of the northern ocean seen in greater perfection, or more safely and easily, than in the Shetland Islands.

One of the finest buildings in Lerwick is the Anderson Institute, presented to the county by Mr. Arthur Anderson, a native of the Shetlands, who represented them in Parliament from 1847 to 1852. It consists of an upper and an elementary school, which are well attended ; the instruction is of a very efficient character. The Widows' Asylum was also erected by Mr. Anderson in 1865, for the benefit of the widows of Shetland sailors and fishermen ; it affords accommodation for about twenty widows and their families, who also have the advantage of a pension fund.

The Shetlanders are hardy and experienced sailors, and many occupy positions of responsibility as officers of even the highest grade on ocean steamships. The Norse characteristics are more manifest here than in the Orkneys, though less than in the Faroes, to which we next proceeded. Though settled first by the Picts, the subsequent Norwegian wave effaced most of the marks now seen in northern Scotland, and the islanders impress you rather as Norwegians than Caledonians. The islands fell to Scotland in the same way and at the same time as the Orkneys; the Scottish monarchy was thus the strongest at its northern extremity, terminating the reign of the Vikings, who held undisputed sway over the northern main for nearly six centuries.

Unst, the most northerly of the British islands, about ten by four miles in extent, also bears traces of the ancient courts of justice, characteristic of the Norsemen. This was probably the first settled by the Scandinavians, and it was at Haraldswick that Harald, the Fair-haired, landed, when on his great expedition, which resulted in the annexation of the Shetlands and the Orkneys to Norway. Before his landing, however, it had been an important Pictish colony, as evinced by the remains of three Druidical circles, of the diameters of 67, 54½, and 40 feet, and in the centre a mound of stones 12 feet in diameter, believed to be part of a temple afterward built by the Scandinavians.

At the head of one of its bays, on a lawn in front of a gentleman's residence, is an upright stone, used by the French astronomer, Biot, for the support of the instrument used by him in 1817 in making observations on the English arc of meridian, for the purpose of determining the figure of the earth by the action of the pendulum. Papa Stour, one of the westernmost islands, is noted as being the place where the Irish monks first introduced Christianity to these islands.

Almost every store in Lerwick is engaged in the selling of the hosiery, veils, and shawls for which the Shetlands are famous, and the runners for the rival establishments put into our hands their handbills before our steamer came to anchor. The fabric is so delicate, and the patterns and colors so pretty, that we could not resist the temptation to invest a pound or two in this bewitching drapery. The Shetland ponies, of which every boy and girl is so covetous, we saw feeding here and there, or carrying various burdens. They are a very small breed, rough-coated from want of care and exposure, but very strong, docile, and gentle. One little fellow, not much bigger than a Newfoundland dog, scampered on before us several miles, bearing on his back his master, a tall, raw-boned islander, whose feet came within a few inches of the ground ; it was the smallest amount of horse to the largest amount of man that I ever saw.

We sailed at 5 P.M. for the Faroe Islands, with a cloudy sky, driving mist, and every prospect of a rainy night, unfavorable wind, and heavy sea, in which we were not disappointed.

CHAPTER III.

THE FAROE ISLANDS.

Rough Seas and Fog. — Dangerous Navigation. — Scenery. — Characteristics of the Faroes. — Early History. — Occupations of the People. — Thorshavn, the Capital. — The Danish Fleet. — Houses, Streets, and Shops. — Living Norsemen. — Reception of the King of Denmark. — Church Service. — A Gala Day. — Start, for Iceland.

> " For all is rock at random thrown,
> Black waves, blue crags, and banks of stone, —
> As if were here denied
> The summer's sun, the spring's sweet dew,
> That clothe with many a varied hue
> The bleakest mountain side."

OUR pilot left us in about two hours, to pursue our unerring course, thanks to good seamanship and the power of steam, through fog and wind and storm, to the Faroes, distant one hundred and eighty-five miles in a north-westerly direction. Darkness was not added to the other dangers, a sort of semi-twilight, in spite of the misty clouds, lasting all night. The sea was very rough, and most of us paid tribute to Neptune, who moreover asserted his victory over me by making me thoroughly uncomfortable ; I was very glad that no importunate newspapers were looking to me for a hurried account of the strange things we saw. In the afternoon we came in sight of the southern island of the group, passing some fine scenery which the occasionally lifting fog enabled us to get glimpses of. As usual, we got lost in the fog, and had to feel our way very slowly among these dangerous rocks, knowing that the strong currents must have taken us somewhat out of our course. We finally were cheered by the sight of the greater Diman, a melancholy-looking rock, about a mile long by half a mile wide, one of the most inaccessible of the group ; even this rocky monster had a pleasant look, as it told us just where we were. The shore is so steep that no boat can be kept there, and the wretched inhabitants are almost shut off from their kind ; the clergyman, who visits them once or twice a year, has to be pulled up by ropes from the cliffs. It is a great place for the breeding of sea-birds, whose young and eggs supply a large part of the food consumed there.

The mountains were, at least, half a mile high, and the cliffs with their base in the sea and their summits in the clouds, with precipitous sides rent by deep and narrow chasms, tenanted by innumerable sea birds, whose harsh voices were louder than those of the wind and waves, were singularly grand and picturesquely dreary.

The Faroe Islands, as far as coast scenery and peo-

ple are concerned, are a sort of Iceland in miniature.
Settled by the same fierce Northmen who were driven
from Norway by Harald, the Fair-haired, their greater
distance from Great Britain, and their consequently
more isolated situation, in connection with the difficulty and danger of reaching them in the foggy and
stormy northern ocean, have given them a peculiar
character, very different from the poetic and literary
Icelanders of the olden time. I say of the olden time,
as at the present day, poetry, literature, and even
ordinary energy have ceased to be characteristic of
the down-trodden, too much governed, Iceland. The
name is derived from *faer*, a sheep. The group rises
from the ocean, between 61° and 62° N. lat., with
high perpendicular cliffs of the wildest character, in-
dented by deep gulfs or bays, and fashioned into the
most fantastic forms, tenanted by innumerable birds.
About twenty out of thirty-five small islands are inhabited, the rest being naked rocks, inaccessible,
except to sea-birds, and daring bird and egg hunters.
The extent of open sea in all directions, three hundred
and twenty miles to Iceland and over four hundred to
Norway, exposes them always to the fury of the waves,
which dash, even in calm weather, with ‚violence
against the rocks ; the water is very deep close to the
shore, and the currents are very strong and dangerous
in the fogs which there abound. The climate is not

severe, being tempered by the ocean ; grass grows at an elevation of 2000 feet, though the mountain tops, some 900 feet higher, are perfectly barren ; the absence of trees here, as well as in Iceland, is due to the high winds and the salt mist, and not to excess of cold. Barley, the only grain which will grow in Faroe, ripens at elevations varying from 80 to 400 feet, according to northern or southern exposure.

The Faroese, though belonging to the same stock as the Icelanders, were never, like them, a literary people, probably, because the population was a very fluctuating one with decided piratical tendencies, most of the early colonists having come from the Loffoden Islands, off the coast of Norway. Though nominally subject to Norway, they were practically independent, refusing to pay tribute, and apparently for a long time forgotten by the mother country, their fierce manners being rendered more peaceful by Catholic Christianity.

From their exposed situation they were frequently plundered by pirates, English, French, and Turkish, though afterwards protected by Denmark, when this country was united to Norway. During our revolutionary war, much of our colonial produce found its way there, whence it was smuggled into Scotland. Being wholly unprotected, during the wars of the northern nations, they suffered great privations from the interruption of trade, to such an extent that England, in 1809 to 1811, allowed them to trade with some of her ports, as stranger-friends, too feeble to act as enemies and powerless as friends. This will account for the extent to which the English language is spoken by the old traders at Thorshavn. In 1814, the peace restored them to Denmark, which has monopolized the small trade ever since, with the usual oppression of monopolies.

Their agricultural products are small, as, from the rocky character of the soil, most of the cultivation must be done with the hoe instead of the plough. Beside the pursuit of the cod and herring fisheries, the taking of seals and whales is an important industry. When a school of dolphins is in sight, the joyful news is communicated by signal fires, and the boats, to the number of several hundred, soon form a huge semicircle around the prey, driving them into shallow water with shouts and blows, where they are quickly killed by the excited crowd. The flesh is eaten fresh and dried, and the blubber, is converted into train-oil for food and various uses. Almost all kinds of seafowl, the gulls and cormorants excepted, are eaten, fresh, salted, or dried, as, also, are their eggs. They raise many cattle, ponies, and sheep, for which the fields are well calculated ; from the latter, as in Iceland, the wool is pulled instead of being shorn, the portions ready to fall being taken at each time. The people are healthy and long lived, but do not increase rapidly.

It was 9 P.M. when we reached the capital, Thorshavn, on the principal island, Stromoe, which contains about one hundred and forty-three square miles, being on an average about twenty-six miles long and nearly six miles wide. These islands were known to the Norwegian rovers before the settlement of Iceland, this last having been discovered by the former toward the end of the ninth century ; they were not chosen for fixed habitations till the wars of Harald drove the chiefs and their followers from Norway to the northern islands. They are now the property of Denmark, and at Thorshavn we found the ships of his Danish majesty, just arrived from Copenhagen on their way to attend the Iceland millennial celebration ; they had put in for the double purpose of taking on coal and of visiting this distant dependency.

We saw the flag of Denmark, a white cross on a scarlet ground, floating from the masts of two men-of-war, from several smaller vessels in the harbor, and from numerous points on shore, which we at first took for grassy hillocks, but afterward discovered to be roofs of turf-covered houses. We had left British waters, and were anchored in the seas once ploughed by the Scandinavian sea-kings. We here first came into contact with a pure Norse people, and first saw the form of house almost universal in Iceland, with low walls and roofs overgrown with grass-bearing turf, hardly distinguishable from the ground about them except for the wreaths of smoke and the flags. It being quite light we went ashore soon after coming to anchor.

The town is situated on the rocky hills surrounding two exposed bays separated by a peninsula ; the houses are placed in utter confusion, wherever intervals between the black rocks or any level surface will permit. This, while it adds in one sense to the picturesqueness as seen from the sea, makes getting about in any definite direction very difficult. There can hardly be said to be any streets, but steep, irregular, narrow, stone-paved lanes, sometimes in front and sometimes in the rear of the houses, and often admitting only persons going in single file ; the pavements were slippery from fish-skin and refuse, and the sides redolent of fish and the slops of the houses ; it reminded me of some of the streets in New York near the wharves and markets. The houses were generally small and miserable, made of wood, tarred to preserve them from dampness, with sod-covered roofs ; the fronts and projecting corners were adorned by strings of fish in every stage of decomposition, the attempt at drying them in such a moist air being,

STREET IN THORSHAVN, FAROES.

according to my nasal organs, often a decided failure. The odors of fish and oil predominated everywhere, and the interior of the houses betokened discomfort, dampness, closeness, and want of cleanliness, which must be a fruitful source of disease and premature death, especially in children. It was a dismal day, and it was to me impossible to associate any idea of home with such dwellings. In some of the better houses, of two or more stories, lace curtains and flowers gave a cheerful look to the windows, and evidences of woman's taste. Though night by the clock, it was light, and the shops were open and crowded. We went into one pestiferous place, through a dark, ill-paved, and winding alley, where we found men drinking in one corner, and in another some women buying gewgaws for the morrow's celebration with all the eagerness, chatter, and apparent satisfaction of a shopper on Broadway. The odor was overpowering from reeking garments, wet shoes, unclean bodies, and the organic and inorganic stock upon the shelves; any thing could be procured here from a needle to an iron chain, from a bit of candy to a pound of snuff, from a keg of fish to a bottle of brandy.

The Norse characteristics of the people were evident at a glance; the abundant light hair and beard, blue eyes, ruddy complexion, tall stature, and stalwart form, revealed the old viking race. The physical appearance and dress of the people were much like those of the Norwegians, and their habits those of fishing communities in high latitudes ; a very little agriculture, a little grazing, and a great deal of fishing, are their occupations. They were very respectful, raising their Phrygian caps as we passed, and bidding us good-evening. The men wore breeches of woollen material, of their own manufacture, buttoned below the knee, and upper garments like northern fishermen ; long woollen stockings and seal-skin shoes, kept from the wet pavement by clattering wooden clogs, completed their attire. I saw nothing peculiar about the female costume ; the inevitable shawl around the shoulders, and a head-dress consisting of a black-silk handkerchief tied behind with a point toward the forehead, were not at all becoming.

Just before our arrival the king had made his official entry, and the harbor was still gay with flags and rushing boats, and the streets were spanned with arches and strewed with flowers. The people in gala dress were quietly watching the processions, and the petty officials were strutting around with all the pomp and feathers of one of our militia trainings. Such an important event as the landing of a king, for the first time since their occupation by Denmark, was deemed

worthy of a formal address by the mayor, but so overpowered was he by the grandeur of the occasion, that
his loyal heart could not bear the emotion, and he fell
dead at the very feet of the king. This, of course,
gave a tone of sadness to what otherwise would have
been universal rejoicing.

The town, named after the god Thor, ordinarily
contains about eight hundred inhabitants, many of
whom are Danes, and this element of the population
was very demonstrative for obvious reasons ; the
place was now crowded with strangers from all parts
of the island to see the king, who had been expected
the day before. His majesty occupied the governor's
house on the hill, and the road thereto from the arch
of welcome on the shore had been strewn with flowers.
His officers were disposed in the houses of the principal residents, to a degree that the operations of the
post-office, the schools, and the courts of justice, were
practically suspended.

Passing the night on board our steamer, as we
always did when in port, we retired at 11 P.M., it still
being quite light. We went ashore the next day, Sunday, to attend church, whither the king and his party
went to participate in a simple, tedious medley of inau-
dible prayer, poor singing, and a prosy sermon in the
Danish language. The wash of the waves made a
landing difficult on the slippery rocks, the only

wharves being irregular heaps of stones ; it required considerable dexterity to avoid getting wet feet and being thrown down ; but friendly hands were extended to save us, and we landed in good condition. Our boats carried the American and English flags, which the people seemed to look at with more enthusiasm than at the Danish.

The crowds were well dressed, and every thing, as yesterday, had a gala look, on land and water, as far as flags could make it. We visited various public buildings and private residences, but could not get access to any officials as all were busy at breakfast with their stranger guests. While waiting for the opening of the church, after looking at the tombstones in the neat church-yard, we ascended a hill behind the useless fort, the only decent walk in the place, and thence had a fine view of the town, its harbor, the gardens and fields of grass and hardy vegetables, and the mist-covered mountains in the distance.

At 11 A.M. we went to the church, where seats had been reserved for us ; it was of the plainest description, with uncushioned seats innocent of paint, accommodating a few hundred persons on the floor and small gallery. The altar, over which was a faded picture of the entombment of Christ, was at the rear of a space raised a few inches above the floor, and in this space seats had been arranged for the king and

his suite. Soon the bells began to ring, the great
doors were thrown open, and the king entered, quietly
walking with the prince Waldemar to his seat, bowing
on each side as he passed along. He was simply
dressed in the Danish naval uniform with a few
decorations·; his appearance was dignified, his expression kind and genial, with an entire absence of that
hauteur and formality which some potentates think
indicate the divinity of royalty. Indeed, had he made
a display, in proportion to that of some of his followers, the islanders would have liked it better, as most
of them looked upon the visit as a mere pageant,
without any political significance or possible benefit
to them.

The audience were quiet and devotional, joining in
the hymns with fervent but unmusical voices. The
women looked care-worn and prematurely old, and I
saw no signs of beauty. There was no pretension to
dress, though upstairs I caught a glimpse of some
Paris-looking hats, doubtless accompanied by three-
button gloves.

As in Iceland, the people here are all Lutherans ;
but the altar, the burning candles, and the dress, atti-
tudes, and tones of the clergyman, gave a semi-Romish
character to the service, at variance with the independent, intelligent character of the audience. I think
all were glad when the ceremony was over, as neither

3   D

fresh ideas nor fresh air were supplied during its continuance. The clergyman was enclosed in a box-like pulpit on one side, high above the heads of his congregation; he looked very queer with his stiff, plaited Elizabethan ruff about his neck. The royal party seemed bored by the platitudes of the sermon, and, at the close of the services, departed, before the audience, with great alacrity.

After the service the king and his party returned to the frigate to dinner, to which many of the people had been invited; the vessel was about two miles from shore, and the sea quite rough, yet boat-load after boat-load, including many ladies, went to and fro all the afternoon and late into the night. Some of the guests, high in church and state, are currently reported to have imbibed more stimulating drinks than were consistent with Sunday gravity or steady loco-motion; judging from the hilarity, and evident dis-arrangement of ruffs, epaulettes, and hats, this may safely be set down as a fact.

The people were admitted to see the tables and the cabins, the former rich with gold and silver, and the lat-ter gaily furnished; the ship was, however, of the old-fashioned type, slow, with many hundred tons of old iron in the shape of cannon, whose space on such a long and rough voyage had much better have been occupied by coal, saving thereby much labor and time.

Among other places, we visited the school, occupied then by the guests, and were pleased to see in this distant island modern apparatus for physical out-door exercise. Living as they do chiefly on barley meal, milk, sheep, fish, and sea-fowl and their eggs, the health of the children is often affected by the foul air of the houses; the school, therefore, not only educates the mind, but does much to invigorate the body.

This gentle-mannered race seemed out of place amid the rugged scenery, bleak rocks, howling winds, and stormy seas of the Faroes; we should rather have expected a coarse, bold, semi-savage horde, as the legitimate descendants of the vikings of old.

The king was everywhere saluted with respect, but not with enthusiasm, except by his Danish subjects; the same indifference I noticed in Iceland. The old Scandinavian independence, almost contempt for royalty, as such, was publicly manifest; they had nothing to ask, and it never entered their heads that a king of Denmark, the first that ever visited these islands, had the inclination, if he had the power, to grant them any political favors. His visit they attributed to curiosity, and they gratified their own at the same time at his expense.

The day had been windy and rainy, and the night was unpromising; we could see that the waves outside were dashing with violence against the rocky shores, and we retired, hoping for a calmer sea the next day. Early the next morning we sailed, in advance of the royal vessels, for Iceland, 320 miles to the north-west, which we ought to reach, wind and weather permitting, in about forty hours.

The Faroese are long-lived, and the climate, notwithstanding its occasional severity and sudden changes, must be a healthy one, or, as in Iceland, the race would long ago have been exterminated by the utter absence of all sanitary precautions to prevent disease.

CHAPTER IV.

OFF FOR ICELAND.

> " Break, break, break,
> On Iceland's cliffs, O Sea !
> How I wish that my tongue could tell
> The thoughts that arose in me,
> O land of mystery !
>
> Break, break, break,
> On her black and jagged rocks ;
> While life shall last, the memory
> Of thy tossing surge, O angry sea !
> Shall ever come back to me."

WE left Thorshavn at 3 A.M., July 27th, the sea being quiet for these latitudes ; the mists had lifted, and, though the sky was as usual overcast, the rocky shores were sufficiently distinct to render navigation for the practised eye easy. The sun bravely battled with the obstructing clouds, and finally obtained the victory, painting the lofty cliffs with beautiful and ever-changing hues. The temperature of

the water was 52° F.; as this was the middle of
summer, we saw nothing of the icebergs and fields
of ice which occur in these seas for the greater part
of the year, cutting off the people of Iceland for several months at a time from intercourse with the rest
of the world. The north-east wind was chilly, and
chased the light clouds in a threatening manner.

We made, however, good progress all day, and con-
gratulated ourselves on the exceptionally pleasant
voyage ; but we reckoned without our host, as there
is no "old probabilities" up there, except the barometer, whose faithful warnings had not yet told us of
the approaching storm. As a prelude to the tempest,
the wind changed to the south, and the warm air and
light of night kept us all on deck. Among the crew
was a fair violinist, who accompanied himself and
others in some sweet and plaintive Scotch and Irish
songs ; his livelier strains, added to those of a well-
played accordion, set the sailors dancing with great
glee for an hour or two.

We had an excellent cook, and, with the good materials at his command, he kept our table supplied
with such palatable viands that, in spite of moderate
and justifiable sea-sickness, we actually enjoyed our
three meals a day. From previous experience I had
made up my mind that brandy, wine, and other stim-
ulants were rather provocative than preventive of

sea-sickness ; and I attribute my comparative freedom from this condition, and my ability to present
myself at table when most others absented themselves, to my almost entire abstinence from spirituous
compounds.

I kept a good lookout for two Scandinavian celebrities of the ocean, the kraken and the sea-serpent.
The former, probably mythical, was a gigantic cephal-
opod, cuttle-fish or squid, whose existence, in a less
exaggerated form, the great squids recently found on
the coast of Newfoundland give good reason to maintain. The idea of a sea-serpent originated in northern
Europe, and was mythological in its first concep-
tion. The Midgard serpent, offspring of Loki, which
girds the world in its folds, and inhabits the deep
ocean till the "twilight of the gods," when it and
Thor will kill each other, plays a conspicuous part in
the Edda ; and the gradual passage of the idea from
mythology to natural history, perhaps from some
creature seen in the northern seas, may be traced in
Olaus Magnus and the later sagas, till the Latin of
bishop Pontoppidan gave it currency in Europe, with
the natural additions of popular fancy. I had more
faith in the sea-serpent ; this was his year for the
northern European seas, as he seems to spend a year
alternating between the Norwegian coast and the
shores of America ; his appearance was chronicled

in Massachusetts Bay in 1873 and again in 1875. No less an authority than the late Professor Agassiz has stated in print his belief in such a creature ; those interested in the subject are referred, for the arguments pro and con, to the " Proceedings of the Boston Society of Natural History," vol. xvi., pp. 337–339, for March 18, 1874. He did not, however, present himself.

We made a good run all night and the next forenoon, and calculated, by dead reckoning and study of the currents and tides, that we could not be far from the southern point of Iceland, and that in a few hours we should see the icy mountains of the region of Skaptar Jokul. The wind began to increase, turning more to the westward, and with it the waves ; the clouds looked black and angry, and the rain drove us all below. The barometer kept falling, and the captain, knowing a gale would soon be upon us, changed his course more to the west, and more in the face of the gale. At midnight we reached the Westmann Islands ; after a severe buffeting from the storm, every thing above and below decks wet, we were glad to sight some low, dark, dismal-looking rocks, against which the waves were dashing furiously ; they were the outliers of the islands, west of the southern point of Iceland. We had hoped to make the Portland Head, more to the eastward, and to see the magnificent arch there perforated in the rock by the incessant blows of the ocean surges driven by wind and tide; it is about sixty feet high and a quarter of a mile wide, affording shelter to innumerable sea-birds, the rock itself rising much higher. Seaward are the isolated, needle-shaped rocks, very dangerous to navigators, as, indeed, is the whole coast of Iceland, there being not a single lighthouse along its immense, fog-bound and tempestuous extent of shore.

These volcanic islands, about fifteen miles from the main-land, are of the most dismal and forbidding aspect; as much cut off from Iceland, as this is from Europe. The few people live on fish and puffins, selling the feathers of the latter to obtain the necessaries of life. Settled by murderers, plundered by pirates, they seem to be very undesirable places of residence, though the soil is said to be fertile, and loved by the inhabitants.

So furious was the gale that we tried to put into the Westmann Islands, sending up rockets and blowing the whistle a long time; but as it was midnight no notice was taken of our signals, and we were forced to breast the gale. Had we sails only, we must have been driven on a lee shore, whose jagged rocks would have instantly destroyed us; but armed with steam we defied the wind and waves, and pushed on our course, though our staunch little craft fairly staggered

3*

under the heavy blows she received, rolling and plung-
ing so that it was quite impossible for any of us to
walk or even stand. The coast was now and then
visible, enabling us to keep at a safe distance. The
gale increased during the night, and in the morning,
I think, the breakfast table was deserted ; the captain
at his post on the bridge, and his passengers tightly
wedged in their berths. We passed a miserable forenoon, but now and then caught a peep of high mountains, and, with the help of a little imagination, of
white glaciers in the interior. At noon we sighted
Cape Reykianess, or Smoky Point, the south-west
corner of Iceland ; skirting along the Faxa fiord, in
about three hours we turned around the northern arm
of the peninsula, and changing then our course to
east, came into smoother water, in sight of green
shores, with here and there a low house ; the view to
the north was bounded by high mountains, among
which we afterward distinguished the famous Jokul,
or ice mountain of Snæfells. At last, the masts of
large vessels, the naval representatives of Denmark,
Norway, Sweden, Germany, and France, and several
smaller craft, showed us that we were in the harbor of
Reykjavik, the capital of Iceland.

Nothing can be more dreary, not to say frightful,
than the coast of Iceland seen through the fog and
rain, and in the teeth of a gale ; nothing can be more

magnificent, when clear weather permits you to look beyond the shore to the shining-white, icy mountains in the interior. The jagged, black, surf-beaten lava rocks tell of the battle between fire and water, which has produced and desolated this island; piled in utter confusion, they break the force of the waves, whose disintegrating power is seen in the pinnacles and arches with which the shore is lined. The most noted of these arches is the barren rock of Dyrholarey (the door) or Portland Head, before alluded to, in which the ocean has perforated an arch, or gateway, large enough for a small vessel to go through; the home of innumerable sea-birds.

In clear weather, which unfortunately is rare in these latitudes, long before the coast is visible, small white clouds appear on the horizon, which soon become the outlines of mountains; and finally are recognized as the magnificent piles of snow-capped peaks, the so-called Jokuls; Snæfells is seen more than one hundred and forty miles from land; and Hekla, glittering in the sun, its internal fires, at present, not powerful enough to melt the snow from its summit, gives you the first grand emotion on visiting Iceland, long before you touch it.

Iceland is somewhat larger than Ireland, and, next to Great Britain, the largest island in Europe; it is in the midst of the Northern Ocean, between $63\frac{1}{2}°$

and 66½° N. lat. (at least 22 degrees farther north than Boston), and between 13° and 24° W. longitude; five hundred miles north-west of Scotland, it is about as far north as Behring's Straits in North America, and the Bay of Trondheim in Norway; in latitude, therefore, corresponding very well with the Alaskan settlement which the Iceland colony in Wisconsin proposed to make. It hardly comes within the arctic circle at its most northern point. Its greatest extent is from east to west, varying from three hundred and twenty to one hundred and eighty miles. About one-ninth of its forty thousand square miles is fit for human habitations, the rest being deserts of snow and ice, lava, and volcanic ashes. It is only about two hundred miles from Greenland, and thus geographically belongs rather to the American conti-nent; but historically and politically it is a part of Europe, though this is three hundred miles more distant.

Our passage to Iceland had been chilly, foggy, and rainy, ending in a furious gale. The approach to a rock-bound coast, in a gale of wind, with no observa-tion of the sun for twenty-four hours and not know-ing how far tidal and other currents had interfered with our reckoning, was not calculated to awaken pleasurable emotions, and we were well pleased, there-fore, after tossing about two days and a half, to come to rest in this quiet harbor, bearing the news of the approach of the king of Denmark, whose fleet arrived the next day at noon.

As we entered the harbor, a boat came alongside, and an Icelander, one of the committee of reception, indicated the place of our anchorage. The anchor was hardly down, when an officer from the Danish steamer boarded us, and politely informed us that we had placed our vessel in the way of the king's ships. Iceland and Denmark had some sharp words on the subject, but gold lace triumphed; America and England, while wondering at the strange antipathy always manifested by the natives against the Danes, quietly raised the anchor again, and took the new position assigned them.

The harbor and the shore presented the same holiday appearance noticed in Thorshavn; the ships of the various nationalities were trimmed with their gayest strings of flags, and the white cross on the scarlet flag of Denmark greeted the eyes in all directions. As we carried the American flag at the foremast and the English at the stern, we excited considerable attention, and everybody wondered where our rakish-looking craft came from out of the jaws of the storm. The picture gives an excellent view of the fleet in the harbor, our steamer occupying a prominent place. We went on shore as soon as possible, heralding the advance of the king, and were cordially received by the authorities.

I had expected to see a dirty, uncomfortable, ill-arranged town, judging from the tales of even the most recent travellers. Whether the visit of the king had caused a change or not, I cannot say, but we found the place tidy, the houses well-built and very pleasant, the streets clean, and every indication of a prosperous, well-ordered, and intelligent community. The shore was lined with boats, the harbor gay with merchant and war vessels, and every thing had a cheerful look, far more so than many of the fishing towns of Scotland and the northern islands. Piles of fish indicated the chief business of the people, and in some cases were not agreeable to the senses of sight and smell ; but the respectful salutations of the citizens, the neatness of their dress, the flowers and other evidences of refinement outside and inside the houses, the crowds in the stores, the trains of ponies, gave me a very good first impression of the capital of Iceland. The houses are of the same style as in the Faroes, the governor's house, the church, and the prison being built of lava blocks, the better ones of wood painted or tarred, and those of the poorer classes of lava and turf, with the roof overgrown with grass.

We lived on board our steamer, remaining quiet

for three days in port, awaiting the beginning of the millennial celebration, which was to last a week, commencing Sunday, August 2. The time passed very pleasantly, visiting the officials, and observing the habits of the people. They are a strange compound of indifference and energy, like their country, which exhibits the coldness and stillness of snow with the fiery activity of the volcano. The society of the capital, chiefly Icelandic, is refined ; their balls showed a beauty of feature and form and elegance of dress which one would hardly expect so near the arctic circle ; the university and public library attract students from all parts of the island, and some of its professors are very learned men, especially in the departments of history and antiquities of the Scandinavian races. Three newspapers in the Icelandic language are published weekly in the capital.

CHAPTER V.

CELEBRATION AT REYKJAVIK.

> " We come, the children of thy Vinland,
>   The youngest of the world's high peers,
> O land of steel and song and saga,
>   To greet thy glorious thousand years !
>
> What though thy native harps be silent,
>   The chord they struck shall ours prolong ;
> We claim thee kindred, call thee mother,
>   O land of saga, steel, and song ! "

NUMEROUS boats were drawn up on the part of the beach at which we landed; we drew up alongside of one of the several piers, long and slanting, the greater portion of which is covered at high tide, which is said to rise here seventeen feet. The streets were level, black from volcanic sand, wider and cleaner than at Thorshavn ; many of the houses

Street in Reykjavik, with the Hospital, 1874.

would do credit to a New-England village, in external appearance and interior arrangement and decoration; we saw all the comforts and many of the luxuries of life, including objects of art, flowers, and instruments of music. The stores were much crowded, and their contents of that miscellaneous character well known in our country towns; here, if anywhere, is a legitimate codfish aristocracy, as these finny inhabitants of the deep are what induce vessels of France and northern nations to cruise in Icelandic waters, enriching by the exchange of commodities the Danish merchants, who have the monopoly of the best trade. Very little idea of the native population can be obtained at the capital, where Danes and other foreigners constitute a large part of the residents; neither the physical, intellectual, nor mental characteristics of the Icelander can be seen to perfection there; we were, however, peculiarly fortunate, as the expected arrival of the king of Denmark had brought them in considerable numbers from the neighboring farms.

We first paid our respects to Governor Finsen, whose house, represented in the picture, was the royal headquarters; he could not give us much attention, and indeed we neither expected nor desired it; he conversed with us in French, but not in English, and promised to secure seats for us in the cathedral on Sunday. I carried several volumes and pamphlets,

E

published by the Boston Society of Natural History
and Institute of Technology, for their public library,
which I presented through Dr. John Hjaltalin, M.D.,
the principal physician of the country, and well versed
in antiquarian and scientific lore; he spoke English
very well, and received us in the most cordial manner; his father was a parish priest mentioned by
Mackenzie, and he himself had studied his profession
at Copenhagen, had visited Scotland, and was well
posted in the various departments of natural science.
He is the "jovial Dr. Hjaltalin" alluded to by Lord
Dufferin, in 1856, in his "Letters from High Latitudes."

On Saturday, August 1, it was chilly, misty, windy,
and rainy. At 10 A.M., when the royal fleet was sig-
nalled, the ships and houses put out all the flags and
streamers they could muster, and the harbor and
shore exhibited a brilliancy of color never seen there
before. Toward noon, the two frigates, with the royal
standard at the mast-head, passed, 'mid the booming
of cannon, through the ranks of the other national
vessels, whose yards were manned in spite of the
rain, to their assigned anchorage. Even the little
"Albion" spoke on this occasion, both for America
and England, with her brass pieces, one of which
turned fairly topsy-turvy in its noisy joy; as ours
did not open their mouths till the grander salutes had

HARBOR OF REYKJAVIK AT THE ARRIVAL OF THE KING.

been paid, their spiteful bark created quite a sensation.

The governor and other officials at once went on board, and in about half an hour the king and his suite entered their boats and went ashore, where a sloping wharf, tastefully decorated, had been built for his landing. After a few formal speeches from the authorities, without the fatal result experienced at Thorshavn, and a faint cheer from the nearest bystanders, the king and his son, Waldemar, walked up the pier amid the respectful, but not cheery demonstrations of the two hundred people in the streets ; they walked in procession to the governor's house, where we will leave them, to receive the various deputations from the citizens, each of which had its little official speech to make, to which a respectful audience and reply were granted.

Reykjavik means "Smoking Harbor," as Reykianess means "Smoking Point," both evincing the fiery agencies once active there ; but both are now misnomers, especially the first, as the warm springs, which gave the name, now give no aërial sign. Some of our party went in search of them, under the guidance of the captain, who had visited them a few years before ; but as they now issue under water they could not be found ; and their natural wash-tub, formerly so convenient to sailors, has well-nigh ceased to exist.

One of the greatest treats we had was the fine salmon of Iceland. Mr. Thomsen, a Danish merchant, has the sole right of fishing in the Lax River ; he has constructed ways leading by small cascades to boxes, up which the frisky fish jump, being therein detained till wanted for use. Some of our party went out there a few miles on horseback, as a first lesson in riding the native ponies, and enjoyed the felicity of scooping up a few fair ones in a net ; the poor creatures could not escape, affording no more sport than taking them out of a tub ; such piscatorial murder could only disgust a lover of the rod and reel. Royalty had scooped the day before, so that the fish obtained on this occasion were not large.

Sunday, August 2, the first day of the millennial celebration, was windy and chilly ; but the sun shone, and the air was so clear that we could distinctly see the Snæfells Jokul, some sixty-five miles distant to the north-west, its icy whiteness beautifully contrasting with the deep blue of the sky.

The week's programme for the celebration was as follows : — First day ; church festival, state dinner, and popular demonstrations in the evening: second day ; formal welcome at Thingvalla, forty miles from the capital: third day ; arrival at the Geysers: fourth day ; inspection of these wonderful hot springs : fifth day ; return to Thingvalla: sixth day ; grand reception and entertainment on the part of the people: seventh day; return to the capital and formal visits: eighth day, Sunday; grand ball, ending the millennial celebration of 1874.

Going on shore about 10 A.M., we at once went to the square where the church is situated. Among the crowd, we saw some of the picturesque helmets and other articles of female costume, described hereafter; the men were dressed very much like the Faroese.

The church was rather an old building of brick, stone, and stucco; dingy and dilapidated; capable of seating some twelve hundred persons; the interior is dismal, the colors faded, and the light and ventilation poor, though in the last two respects not so bad as some costly modern churches, whose congregations evidently think that a dim religious light adds to the solemnity befitting a sacred edifice. Thorwaldsen, the famous sculptor, claimed by Denmark, was the son of an Icelander, born at sea, Nov. 19, 1770; and a baptismal font made and presented by him in token of his birth, in no way beautiful, is the only note-worthy object in the cathedral.

Having seats reserved for us, we had good opportunity to see the national costume, and especially the helmet-like head dresses and gaily embroidered jackets and veils of the women. The services were of the same semi-Romish, semi-Lutheran character as at the

Faroes, and in the sermon the berobed and beruffed bishop seemed to have a hard struggle between the dignity of the occasion and the consequences of a nose full of snuff, whose visible manifestations were two dark-colored streams from his nostrils, which, carried away by the fervor of his eloquence, he did not always succeed in arresting before they became conspicuous.

I understood not a word of the sermon, and there was no appearance of interest or attention in the audience; I understood hardly any thing of the hymns sung, and yet I do not remember of ever having been so affected by music; sweet, solemn, and slightly plaintive, the chorus of "Iceland's thousand years," words and music of Icelandic origin, brought tears into most eyes, and I am sure it did into mine.

The following is a copy of the Millennial Hymn sung in the church, the words by Matthias Jochumson, and the music by Svb. Sveinbjörnsson.

lof-um þitt hei - lag - a, hei - lag - a nafn. Ur
praise thy ho - ly, ho - ly name. From

sól - ker-fum himn-ann-a knyt-a þjer krans, þinir
solar systems of the heavens wind thee a wreath, thy

her - skar-ar, tim ann - a safn. Fyr - ir
le - gions the times' col - lec - tions. Be - fore

þjer er einn dag - ur sem þús - und ár og
thee is one day as thousand years, and

þús - und ár dag - ur, ei   meir,   eitt
thousand years one day, not more,   one

ei - lífd   ar smá-blóm med titr - and - i tár, sem
eter - nity's small flower with quiver - ing tears which

til - bid - ur gud sinn og deyr.   Is-lands
a - dores   its   God and dies.   Iceland's

þúsund   ár, Is-lands þúsund   ar   eitt
thousand years, Iceland's thousand years   one

ei - lífd - ar smá-blóm med titr - and - i   tár, sem
e - ternity's small flower with quiv-er-ing tear which

til - bid - ur gud sinn og deyr.
wor - ships   its God and dies.

The following are two other verses and their translation: the sign 'þ' is pronounced like 'th.'

2.

O gud, ó gud! vèr föllum fram
Og fórnum þer | : brennandi : | sál,
Gud fadir, vor drottinn frá kyni til kyns,
Og kvökum vort helgasta mal ;
Vjer kvökum og þökkum í þusund ár,
þvi þú ert vort einasta skjól ;
Vjer kvökum og þökkum med titrandi tár,
þvi þú tilbjóst vort forlaga hjól.
| : Islands þusund ár : |
Voru morgunsins húmköldu hrynjandi tár,
Sem hitna vid skinandi sól.

4

3.

O gud vors lands, ó lands vors gud !
Vjer lifum sem | : blaktandi : | strá.
Vjer deyjum ef þú ert ei ljós þad og lif,
Sem ad lyptir oss duþtinu frá.
O vert þu hvern morgun vort ljúfasta lif
Og vor leidogi' i daganna þraut,
Og á kvöldin vor,himneska hvild og vor hlif,
Og vor hertogi a þjódlifsins braut.
   | : Islands þusund ár : |
Verdi gróandi þjódlif med þverrandi tár,
Sem þroskast á gudsrikis braut.

2.

O God, O God, we fall prostrate
And offer Thee our burning soul :
God father, our Lord from kin to kin
And cry our holiest speech ;
We cry (have cried) and we thank (ed) for thousand years
For Thou art our only defence ;
We cry, and we thank with our quivering tears,
For Thou madest the wheel of our fate.
   Iceland's thousand years
Were the morning's chilly and down-flowing tears
Which warm up by the shining sun.

3.

O God of our land, O our land's God !
We live as trembling straws.
We die if Thou art not our light, and the life
Which lifts us up from the dust.
O be Thou each morning our sweetest life,
And our guide through the trouble of days ;
And at eve be our heavenly rest and our shield ;
And our captain through our national path.
   Iceland's thousand years,
Be they a growing, a national life, with lessening tears,
And may it increase on the heavenly kingdom's path.

After the services in the church, the people dispersed, most of them going to the hill of Oskjuhlid, about three miles from town, where addresses, historical reminiscences, songs, dances, and fireworks, were to conclude the day. The king gave a dinner in the afternoon, to which most of our party were invited, and such of them as had swallow-tails and white chokers went thereto ; by some carelessness or inattention they were not introduced individually, but simply as American guests. They were politely and graciously received, and the dinner passed off admirably ; being indisposed, I did not go, and so cannot give any details. My invitation ran as follows :

IFOLGE ALLERHÖIESTE BEFALING TILSIGES

HR. DR. SAMUEL KNEELAND

TIL TAFFEL HOS HANS MAJESTÆT KONGEN,

D. 2 AUGUST 1874, KL. 4.

HOLTEN.

PAAKLÆDNINGEN : GALA.

Every thing, even to the dishes, it is said, came from Copenhagen, so that it was in no sense, except geographically, an Icelandic dinner, unlike the one given by the people to the king at Thingvalla.

After the dinner, the king expressed his gratification at the manner in which the people had received him, and the hope that the country would begin a new era of development from the operation of the new constitution which had been given to it. He then rose, and gave as a toast, "Long live old Iceland," at which cheering from the guests, music from the band, and the roar of cannon from the ships, mingled in patriotic and not discordant sound. Other sentiments followed, with social intercourse ; and then the host and his guests departed from the University building, where the dinner had been given, to the hill where the evening celebration was to take place.

Everybody walked ; the road was good, but the surroundings were dismal in the extreme ; along the gently sloping hill were walking parties of men and women, mostly in holiday attire, toward the barren summit now gay with flags, tents, and many-colored dresses. We toiled along with the rest, and in about an hour, at 7 P.M., reached the top, where over a thousand people were assembled. Some were congregated about the stands for speeches, others were dancing to rude music (and this on Sunday night too), while most were lounging listlessly about, trying to appear to be having a good time.

On the arrival of the king, native songs and speeches followed in quick succession, the former very pleasing in their melody, and the latter patriotic and no doubt satisfactory to those who understood them. All the northern nations of Europe were represented except Great Britain; this last was to me astonishing in view of the fact that the future queen of England, beloved by the nation, is the daughter of Christian the Ninth of Denmark.

The everywhere-present, irrepressible American, received honorable mention and enthusiastic reception for stanzas composed by Bayard Taylor, one of the "American Expeditionists." It came about in this wise, in his own words : "Two days ago we were discussing, in the cabin of our steamer, the question whether we, in our capacity as Americans, should make even an unofficial representation at this festival. We knew that the Icelanders desired that our presence, which seemed to be welcome to them, should be in some way manifested; yet it seemed difficult to decide how this should be done. The proposal, on my part, to address a poetic greeting to Iceland, was so cordially received by my companions that I could only comply. The stanzas which follow were written in all haste, in the midst of distracting talk, and make no claim to any poetic merit."

They are entitled "America to Iceland ;" the first and last stanzas are at the head of this chapter.

> " We come, the children of thy Vinland,
>   The youngest of the world's high peers,
>   O land of steel, and song, and saga,
>   To greet thy glorious thousand years.

Across that sea the son of Erik
    Dared with his venturous dragon's prow;
From shores where Thorfinn set thy banner
    Their latest children seek thee now.

Hail, mother land of skalds and heroes,
    By love of freedom hither hurled;
Fire in their hearts as in thy mountains,
    And strength like thine to shake the world!

When war and ravage wrecked the nations,
    The bird of song made thee her home;
The ancient gods, the ancient glory,
    Still dwelt within thy shores of foam.

Here, as a fount may keep its virtue
    While all the rivers turbid run,
The manly growth of deed and daring
    Was thine beneath a scantier sun.

Set far apart, neglected, exiled,
    Thy children wrote their runes of pride,
With power that brings, in this thy triumph,
    The conquering nations to thy side.

What though thy native harps be silent?
    The chord they struck shall ours prolong;
We claim thee kindred, call thee mother,
    O land of saga, steel, and song!"

Here also is the translation into Icelandic verse by
Matthias Jochumsson.   Notice will here be taken of
the first letter of the fourth word in the first line,
which represents our "th."

AMERIKA TIL ISLANDS.

Hèr koma börn þíns bjarta Vínlands,
Sem byggjum yngstu heimsins grund,
Þú ættland kappa, söngs og sögu,
Að signa þig á frægðarstund!

Vèr hleyptum skeið, þar Eiríks arfi,
Hinn ógnum-prúði sigla nam;
Og þar sem fánar þorfinns gnæfðu,
Vèr þorfinns niðjar, settum fram.

Heill, heill þèr móðir hetjú skálda,
Er hingað leiddi frelsis-orð,
Með eld sem þú í efldum barmi,
Og afl sem þú að bifa storð!

Þá trylltur ofsi eyddi þjóðum,
Nam andans svanur hèr sín lönd,
Og heiðin goð og frægðin forna
Hèr festu byggð á sæbrims-strönd.

Og eins og lindin hrein sèr heldur,
Þótt hlaupi á akra leirug flóð,
Þitt afl og ljós og lífsins dugur
Hèr lifði á sólar-kaldri slóð.

Þótt gleymd, og hrjáð og hrakin værir,
Þín hetjuþjóð skóp fræðar rún,
Er seiðir til þín sigurþjóðir
Að sjá í dag þín frægu tún.

Og þótt þín harpa þagna eigi,
Skal þjóð vor lengja brostin ljóð:
Vèr köllum land þitt kynland, móðir,
Þú kappa, skálda, sögu þjóð!

This probably gave more satisfaction to the people than any other feature of the ceremonies of the day. In their republican independence, they loved not kings, and looked with silent indifference on the provisions of the new constitution, which they would not regard as a boon, claiming it and more as a right; but they would not ignore the fact that a party of American republicans had come nearly four thousand miles to be present at their millennial celebration, and to offer in this way the greetings of the youngest to one of the oldest of the northern nations. The historical connection of Iceland with America long before the discovery of Columbus, and the possible emigration of some of the present inhabitants to our northwest coast, — the Iceland of America, — an exodus which will be increased and hastened by the terrible volcanic eruption of 1875, — made this occasion especially interesting. The poem and subsequent speech by Mr. Taylor, who was introduced as the " Skald from America," were received with the greatest enthusiasm of the day ; and the halo which surrounded his head reflected a few beams on his prosaic companions.

There was nothing peculiar in the dances, which resembled the modern hugging and hopping gymnastics called waltzes, polkas, mazurkas, &c. ; with much activity there was not much grace, and the music was not of an inspiring character; still the picturesque head-dresses, the rosy complexions, and the luxuriant hair of the dancers, made it a scene very pleasant to contemplate.

The wind was keen and strong, and it required a good deal of imagination to call it amusement at a temperature in which an overcoat was decidedly comfortable; yet the girls, in their white dresses, flitted about as ours would at a July picnic. His majesty and suite soon departed for the city, and we for our steamer, to rest and get ready on the morrow to take a horseback ride of ninety miles into the interior as far as the Geysers. The way back was tedious, as we were cold and tired; hardly any thing but bleak and barren stone-covered hills and fields met the sight; the ocean in front and the distant volcanic hills behind us; huge piles of peat drying in the sun for winter fuel added to the blackness of the landscape; not a vestige of human habitation till we came to the city, and then the observatory (unused) and the jail (unoccupied) were the most prominent features. The jail, of stone, one of the finest buildings in the place, has never had an occupant, and, apparently, was built so strongly to keep the poorly housed fishermen from breaking into it and enjoying its comfortable quarters. This speaks well for the community, whose harmless character is also vouched for by the fact that, in a

4*   F

place of fifteen hundred inhabitants, there is one policeman, or watchman, in winter, and two in summer, when wicked foreigners visit their distant shores.

Nothing occurred to mar the happiness of the day, except the severe wounding of two gunners by the premature explosion of a hand grenade among the lava rocks.

We did not wait to see the fireworks at 11½ P.M. I have a good-sized handbill announcing the order and method of performance, of which the following is a translation, line for line :—

NATION'S HIGH TIDE (THJODHATID)

AT OSKJUHLID (BASKET SLOPE HILL),

ON SUNDAY, AUGUST 2, 1874,

AT 3½ P.M.

The people will gather together at the east wall (Austurvelli), and go thence in procession, six abreast, to the place of festival.

From 4 to 6½ o'clock,

SPEECHES AND SONGS.

From 6½ to 11½,

AMUSEMENTS, such as SONGS, MUSIC, DANCING, &c.

From 11½,

FIREWORKS (Flugeldar Miklir), literally great flying fires.

Each one who wishes to be inside the cleared space must wear a badge, which costs 16 skillings (8 cents).

And so ended the first day of the Iceland Millennial.

CHAPTER VI.

PHYSICAL CHARACTERS OF ICELAND.

THE NORTHERN ICE. — BLOCKADE OF THE NORTH SHORE. — CLIMATE. — SAFEGUARD OF NORTHERN EUROPE. — CHAINS OF JOKULS OR SNOWY MOUNTAINS. — GLACIERS. — VOLCANIC ORIGIN OF ISLAND. — FIORDS AND SETTLEMENTS. — DIFFICULT TRAVELLING. — DESERT OF ICELAND. — RIVERS. — WATERFALLS. — LAKES. — NORTH COAST. — NORTH-WESTERN PENINSULA. — RELIGIOUS IDEAS AS INFLUENCED BY PHYSICAL CHARACTERS OF A COUNTRY. — THE OLYMPUS OF JUPITER AND WALHALLA OF THOR.

> " Land of volcano and of fire,
>   Of icy mountains, deserts hoar,
>   Of roaring floods, and earthquakes dire,
>   And legendary lore !
>   Land of a thousand sea-kings' graves, —
>   Those tameless spirits of the past,
>   Fierce as their subject arctic waves,
>   Or hyperborean blast, —
>   The polar billows round thee foam,
>   O Iceland ! long the Norsemen's home."

BEFORE describing our journey into the interior, some account of the physical characters of Iceland will render the subsequent chapters more interesting and intelligible.

It had been my hope, when I left America, ignorant of the subsequent composition of our party, to go north, before the celebration, as far as the island of

Jan Meyen, in lat. 71°, and to the region of the midnight sun, for which at southern Iceland we were a
little too late. We were informed by the captain of
the Danish frigate on the station, just returned from
the north-west of the island, that the northern coast
was so blocked by ice that it would be dangerous, if
not impossible, for us to penetrate to the north in
that direction; the necessary abandonment of that
part of our trip, from this and other causes, led me to
investigate the relation of the geographical position
of Iceland to the movements of the polar ice; and I
found in a communication from Baron Letourneur,
the commander-in-chief of the French navy in Iceland, some very interesting observations on this subject made by him during two consecutive summers.

A glance at the map will show that Iceland, from
a civilized point of view, is the highest inhabitable
and most remarkable meteorological position on the
globe, — on the line of separation between the two
great oceanic currents of this region, the cold waters
from the north going south, and the warm waters of
the gulf stream going north, and at precisely the
point where these two great currents act together
with the greatest energy. For one thousand years,
just terminated, Iceland has been the advanced sen-
tinel of political and intellectual progress in Europe,
it should now add meteorology to the list of its culti-

vated sciences. When the sun in winter leaves these regions, the great depression of temperature forms the immense icy barrier which extends from Greenland to Jan Meyen, Spitzbergen, and Nova Zembla; and Iceland is embraced in the south portion of this field, isolated and unapproachable at this season, hardly even sustaining the lives of its people, without aid from the products of more favored lands.

As soon as the sun rises in the northern hemisphere, and the air gradually becomes warmer, loud crackings in the ice announce its breaking up and its commencing movements, which are hastened by the fierce storms from the south which then prevail. Carried south by the polar current, they reach Iceland in the beginning of spring; the larger and more detached masses moving slowly over an immense extent, meeting more obstacles from the land toward the south, arrest the masses to the north, until the pressure is so great that they precipitate themselves on the north coast of Iceland with terrible force.

For a short time the passage between Greenland and Iceland is obstructed, and the latter is then blocked on the north-west also, and sometimes with such a depression of temperature that the detached ice is again frozen into a solid sheet.

Here Iceland performs its first important office in the physics and meteorology of the globe; it arrests the destructive mass of the polar ice, and allows the establishment of the currents in their normal direction, receiving and moderating the intense cold and the consequent storms. As soon as the obstruction is complete, the waters from the north press upon the accumulated ice, while those from the south, arrested at the north-west point of the island, undermine and eat away the opposing ice, and soon hollow out a passage, through which the accumulated waters from the north rush with violence, carrying with them the ice which blocked Iceland; thence the masses are floated south by the currents, tides, and winds, and gradually melt in the warmer water. Those which are below Langaness do not participate in this movement, and here the ice remains for a longer period.

This is the usual course of the ice, which begins to move in spring, with successive arrivals till the end of summer, when the thaw ceases, and it is seen no more until the next spring; but occasionally, as in 1873–74, a considerable movement occurs in the winter.

If we consider the immense extent of the icy mass thus put in motion, we readily understand the great climatic changes which must result. On the 14th and 15th of April, 1874, occurred, from this cause, the most violent storm remembered on the island, extending over a distance of more than one thousand miles from north to south, and probably to within a few degrees of the North Pole.

The coldness of their winter depends mainly on the formation of the Greenland ice; when the large masses are arrested by Iceland their summers are cold, and those of northern Europe warm; when they float off to the south, the season is mild in Iceland, as the gulf stream gets farther north, and the summer of England and northern Europe is cold. The average temperature at Reykjavik is about that of Moscow, — in summer ranging from 53° to 75° F., and in winter, 29°; average for the year, 39°: at Akureyri, in the north, in summer, 45°; in winter, 20°; and for the year, 32°: but, in the north, the temperature may rise to 75° and fall to 29° below zero.

The geographical position of Iceland is, therefore, very important, as, with Jan Meyen and Spitzbergen, it forms a natural barrier against the desolation of northern Europe by the ice from the arctic regions; should Iceland disappear beneath the waters, Norway would have the cold of Greenland, the north of England would become frozen, and Greenland would be green again. There is geological evidence that Iceland was uplifted toward the end of the glacial epoch of northern Europe, and this would explain the traces of a milder climate, as indicated by plant and animal life, in Greenland, before the advent of man. Indeed, from some cause not well determined, we have reason to believe that Greenland has been green, and that Iceland possessed forests, even within the historic period ; the complete disappearance of the Norse colonies in Greenland in the fifteenth century, and the repeated allusions in the Icelandic sagas to a vegetation now unknown there, seem to show that the climate has become more severe than when the Norsemen sought there a shelter from the persecutions of Harald, the Fair-haired, a contemporary of king Alfred of England. It is almost certain that the climate has undergone a great change, even during the historic period, caused doubtless by the accumulation of the polar ice, and the consequent increase of the snowy jokuls, and with them a diminution of temperature. According to their sagas, grain formerly grew in Iceland, and trees of considerable size; their trunks are found imbedded in the morasses, and houses and even ships in comparatively modern times are said to have been built of native timber.. There have probably been several alternating epochs of cold and heat, corresponding to the varying amount and extent of the ice in the different glacial epochs which modern geology has indicated in northern Europe.

The snowy mountains, or jokuls, are seen, in clear

weather, many miles at sea; though, compared with
the Alps, they are insignificant, the highest being
only five thousand feet high, yet, as they rise almost
from the level of the sea, their masses seem stupen-
dous. Their production depends on the same causes
as the glaciers of the Alps, from snow and the condensed fogs; the outlines are generally rounded, the
surface of the underlying trachytic rock having been
subjected to the eroding and polishing forces of the
ice during the glacial period. They have the slow,
irresistible march of all such great bodies of ice,
gradually invading the plains and dooming large
tracts of land to sterility, removable only by some
great geological change. It must be remembered
that many of these jokuls are slumbering volcanoes,
the ever-present heat from which melts the lower
strata of snow, sometimes deluging the valleys and
pasture-lands with immense floods of water and fragments of ice; the streams which pour from these
jokuls constitute the short, furious, and icy cold rivers
which the traveller has so often to ford.

These jokuls form two nearly parallel chains, separated by a deep valley, in a direction from south-west
to north-east, and on this geological condition depends not only the physical, but the political and
civil condition of the country. The most extensive
and best-known of these chains is on the east, south,

and south-east of the island, not far from the coast,
the highest summits being nearly six thousand feet
high, and those in the south being the first seen on
approaching Iceland, even at a distance of one hundred miles ; the length of this range is more than
two hundred miles. The other chain is more to the
north-west, and less well known, except in the region
of Thingvalla, whose grand but frightful scenery will
be described in a subsequent chapter ; it is about
one hundred and twenty miles long, and of an average
height of five thousand feet ; Mt. Hekla belongs to
neither, being between them at their western extremity, and commanding a view of both.

Snæfells (probably the Sneffels of Jules Verne in
his journey to the centre of the earth), an extinct volcano, between the Breida and Faxa fiords, is covered
with perpetual snow ; from its isolated position, though
only five thousand feet high, its appearance is magnificent ; it is plainly visible from Reykjavik, distant sixty
miles.   From its situation on this long tongue of land,
it seems to spring from mid ocean ; its snowy white
mass against the deep blue sky, is one of the most
beautiful of objects.

All the region between these two fiords is Iceland's classic ground, and the scenes of some of the
most cherished sagas of the country. Almost every
writer on Iceland has given one or two, and espe-

cially Baring Gould in his "Myths of the Middle Ages," 1872, and Prof. Anderson in 1875.

In order to understand the peculiar scenery of Iceland, it should be remembered that its nucleus was thrown up from an almost fathomless ocean by volcanic power ; born of fire, it bid defiance to the waves, and maintained and still preserves its volcanic energy in spite of polar cold and overwhelming ice. It is forty thousand square miles in extent, in shape like a flattened arch, nowhere more than two thousand three hundred feet high ; chiefly basaltic rock and silicious tufa formed beneath the sea ; the former the oldest and the foundation, probably uplifted toward the end of the tertiary period ; the latter formed during the succeeding or glacial epoch ; the lavas were then poured out, entirely above the sea, in and through the trachytic tufa, which goes through the island from south-west to north-east, as before stated, this having evidently been the line of subterranean force.

Some of the most characteristic scenery of Iceland is found in this ocean-born basalt, analogous but inferior to the "Fingal's Cave" and "Giant's Causeway." Near Stappen, in the vicinity of Snæffels, are two very singular obelisks of rock rising from the sea, the higher of which is two hundred and forty feet, and only thirty-five feet wide at the base ; these, and other fantastic forms and caverns, have been fashioned by the waves.

According to Paijkull, a Swedish geologist, who has travelled extensively in Iceland within the last ten years, the form of the country, as it now exists, its rent and uneven surfaces, are due to the action of glaciers. The basaltic rocks show numerous marks of glacial action ; where a deep valley or fiord is seen, there was once a continuous layer of rock, afterward carried away by the ice ; lava, which once must have flowed in horizontal strata of uniform thickness, now appears in hills and undulations, often overlaid by a thick soil ; the erosion of the glacier has done this, and very extensively.

The rocky fissures, or fiords, which extend from the rocky coast far into the interior, are characteristic of Icelandic, as of Norwegian, scenery. Originating perhaps in the fissures of the primary upheaval, extending far beneath the water, they have since been greatly modified by the action of glaciers, the sea, the rains, and the frosts ; they are very narrow in proportion to their length, and resemble rivers with high perpendicular rocky walls. Bare of vegetation, lifeless and still, except from the roar of the wind, the torrent, and the sea, they are inexpressibly grand and gloomy. Yet these rocky wastes, so desolate when viewed from the ocean, are the favorite dwelling-places of the Icelander; here he finds an inexhaustible supply of fish, a plenty of drift-wood for domestic uses, an occasional stranded whale, and a comparatively quiet harbor; the lateral valleys, also the effect of erosion by ice, are apt to be fertile, communicating with grassy meadows well-suited for his cattle. In the neighborhood of these fiords, therefore, we find the thickest-settled portions of the country. It was from one of these fiords, the Breida on the western coast, about one hundred miles north of the capital, that Erik the Red sailed in 984 for the discovery of Greenland.

This structure of the coast, extending as it does far into the interior, facilitates communication by water, but renders travelling by land difficult and often dangerous; the steepness of the ascent and descent; the sudden transition from the heat of the valley to the snow, rain, and wind of the heights; the passage of the narrow bridle-paths along the almost perpendicular sides of precipices whose bases are washed by the sea hundreds of feet below, — unite to make travelling outside of the capital, without a guide, rather a perilous undertaking.

Between the two snowy chains which traverse the country from south-west to north-east lies the "desert" of Iceland, — a mythical land, peopled by the superstitious Northmen by demons, giants, and wild

men, whose deeds have been chronicled in the sagas
which even now form the delight of all classes. It
is a lonely and desolate region, torn by earthquakes,
overwhelmed by lava streams, — as far as known, consisting mainly of large tracts of volcanic sand, destitute of water and without vegetation ; it probably
cannot be exceeded in desolation by any other region
of the earth, and, from its craters, chasms, and blocks
of lava, reminds one of the landscapes figured by astronomers as occurring in the moon, or like an unfin-
ished corner of the universe, where the chaos of the
primeval world still exists, deluged by lavas, mud,
cinders, and water bearing immense blocks of ice, —
thirty thousand square miles of indescribable desolation. In fact, it is a popular saying that Lucifer, at
the beginning of the world, requested permission to
try his hand at creation ; and that, from the fragments left by the antagonism of fire and water, the
unused and useless remnants of the volcano and the
earthquake, he made Iceland, and was well satisfied
with his work. From what I have seen of it, and
from the observations of others, I must say that "diabolic" or "devilish" is the best epithet to express
the character of the scenery. It is just such a place
as Von Weber would have selected for the demon
scenes of his "Der Freischütz," or Salvator Rosa for
his dismal and characteristic paintings.

This desert, an elevated plateau, extending across the island, and about one hundred miles from south to north, is rarely visited by travellers, and by the natives only in the summer, when the women form their tent villages on its borders, while they gather the Iceland moss. There must, however, be fertile districts in it, and the reports, well authenticated, of herds of reindeer issuing from it, and of wild-looking men having horses shod with horn, prove that it is not entirely unsuited for human habitation.

Reindeer were introduced from Norway about 1770; there are considerable herds in the unpopulated districts, especially in the mountain deserts of the northeast; they feed upon the moss, and are pursued with difficulty, as there is no food for horses in their haunts; they are hunted for their flesh, skin, and horns; they are not domesticated, as the country is too rough for their use in sledges. Yet with all its dreariness, and cold, and barrenness, and poverty, and isolation, the people are extremely fond of their country, and say that "Iceland is the fairest land that the sun shines upon." Of them it may be said with Goldsmith : —

> "The shudd'ring tenant of the frigid zone
> Boldly proclaims that happiest spot his own ;
> Extols the treasures of his stormy seas,
> And his long nights of revelry and ease."

Running up from these fiords are numerous rivers,

generally short, furious, and cold, the result of the
melting of the glaciers ; none more than one hundred
miles long, they are not navigable for any great, continuous extent, and oppose formidable obstacles to
the traveller in whatever direction he may go ; twenty
to thirty of these, with their tributaries, he will ford
in the course of the day, shallow, cold, and clear ;
bridges there are none, and very few boats, so that
difficulty and danger both to horse and rider attend
their crossing, whether by fording or swimming ; we
encountered none reaching above the horse's belly.
From the broken nature of the country, they form
several fine waterfalls, one of the prettiest of which is
made by the river Oxer falling over the precipices of
the Almannagja, in the crater-like depression at Thingvalla, where the principal ceremonies of the Millennial celebration took place.   This fall is about eighty
feet high, and visible for many miles, its snowy whiteness being remarkably contrasted against the black
lava rocks over which it flows ; into a deep pool, near
the base of this fall, women found guilty of child-
murder were in old times thrown from the summit of
the precipice ; it is a frightful-looking place, causing
an involuntary shudder as you gaze into its black
depths ; justice in those days was both stern and
speedy.   Another beautiful fall is the Skogafoss, two
hundred feet high, on the south coast, about eighty
miles from the capital.

The lakes of Iceland, from the broken nature of the country, are few; all are situated in the midst of the most desolate scenery, and their sides and bottoms are rough with the lava blocks from the surrounding volcanoes. The largest is Thingvalla lake, along which we journeyed for many hours, near which was formerly held the meetings of the Althing during the independent age of the island; it is clear, cold, very deep, abounding in fish, and visited by innumerable water-fowl; within a century it has been much changed by earthquakes; it is about twelve miles long and five wide, receives the river Oxera, and, it is said, communicates with the sea. It is situated in a magnificent basin in the lava rocks, and the contrast between the black ruggedness of the rim, and the clear green waters of its expanse, with the great, many-hued hills in the distance casting their shadows, and the fleecy clouds mirrored in its surface, make a scene of singular weird-like beauty.

I cannot understand the statements of travellers, and very recent ones too, that there is an entire absence of color in Iceland; it seemed to me just the opposite. The silver pyramids of the jokuls with their glittering mantles of snow, the blackness of the lava, the golden-hued hills in the sunlight, the purple shadows of the precipices, the green of the fields near the shore, the lividity even of the storm-clouds, the blue of the distant ocean, and the still deeper hue of the sky, showed to my eyes the most striking and beautiful contrasts ; we might have been, however, peculiarly fortunate in the weather.

The northern coast of Iceland, which we could not reach on account of the ice on the north-west, though a little colder, is really the most desirable part of the island for habitations ; the soil is deeper, the vegetation more luxuriant and reaching farther up the mountains, which are freèr from snow than in the south and west. The fiords are more accessible and better stocked with fish. Husavik is a considerable trading-town, and where Gardar landed, and passed a winter, in 864, ten years before the permanent settlement on the west coast, whose thousandth anniversary was celebrated in 1874.

Akureyri, on the north coast, is, next to Reykjavik, the most important town in the island ; it has an excellent harbor, and is a miniature copy of the capital. In an old church on the hill is a curious statue carved out of wood, of the size of life, believed to represent St. Olaf, the introducer of Christianity, trampling with his right foot on the neck of a prostrate heathen.

The north-west peninsula of Iceland, rarely visited on account of the difficulty of getting through the ice which generally besets the west coast, is almost an island, the neck which makes it a peninsula being quite narrow. It has been likened to a huge hand, whose wide-spread and numerous fingers touch the arctic zone ; between these outstretched giant fingers run up arms of the sea through peculiarly gloomy fiords, sometimes forty miles long. Grand and fearful always, here they are especially gloomy, enveloped in fogs, cold and boisterous, openings, with the help of a little imagination, always excited by Scandinavian myths, into unknown and mysterious dangers, rendered doubly dreary from the precipices suddenly receding in the gray atmosphere so characteristic of the arctic regions, where the sky, in stormy weather, has been aptly compared to an inverted pewter cup.

It is interesting to trace the natural connection between the physical characters of a barbarous country and the religious ideas of its people. I had before noticed the horrible superstitions of the old Sandwich Islanders, whose principal goddess, Pélé, resided in the fiery depths of Kilauea, and whose vengeful spirit was exhibited in the volcanic eruptions which have so convulsed Hawaii, even to the present time. The attendant and inferior deities typified the antagonism between the ocean and the volcano, the earthquake and the lava stream being the implements and the evidence of the struggle ; to propitiate these gods, whom they saw in the war of the elements around them, thousands of human victims were annually sacrificed. In like manner, amid the rugged scenery of Iceland, we should not expect to find the refinements of artistic Greece and luxurious Rome ; the Norsemen, brought into daily contact with most frightful physical strife, totally unlike the sunny softness of southern Europe, could not be content with the effeminate gods of Olympus, but deified what to them was most necessary ; strength, courage, and endurance, instead of beauty and sensuality, were the qualities that gained access to the Walhalla of the followers of Thor and Odin. The Olympian Jupiter is the effeminate representative of the Scandinavian Thor, — both thunderers, kings of the gods, and rulers of the nations, but as different as the rugged north is from the lascivious south.

In the words of another, " How out of place would seem a Jove, with his beard in ringlets, a trim Apollo, a sleek Bacchus, an ambrosial Venus, a slim Diana, and all their attendant groups of oreads and cupids, amid the ocean mists and ice-bound torrents, the flame-scarred mountains, and four months' night, of a land which the opposing forces of heat and cold have selected for a battle-field ! "

CHAPTER VII.

THE VALLEY OF THINGVALLA.

THINGVALLA. — TRAVELLING IN ICELAND. — HORSES, AND THEIR
LOADING. — RIVERS. — LAVA ROADS. — CHARACTER OF COUNTRY.
— FARM-HOUSES. — NOON STOP. — LAKE OF THINGVALLA. —
CHASM OF ALMANNAGJA. — MANNER OF ITS FORMATION. — EN-
TRANCE TO VALLEY. — ENCAMPMENT.

> " Where, undissolving from the first of time,
> Snows swell on snows amazing to the sky ;
> And icy mountains high on mountains piled
> Seem to the wondering traveller from afar
> Shapeless and white, an atmosphere of clouds,
> Projected huge and horrid o'er the land ;
> While at his feet volcanic blackness reigns,
> And rugged lava blocks the devious way."

THE chief celebration of the millennial was to be
in the valley of Thingvalla, distant about forty
miles from Reykjavik in an easterly direction. This
is the holy ground of Iceland, rendered sacred to
the people by the associations clinging around it as
the scene of the deliberations of their Althing, or
national council, during the days of the republic.
The word means the "plains of the council" or
"thing," and is the same as Dingwall and Tingwall
in Great Britain and its islands. The different spell-

ings of the name depend upon the case used by the writer ; the most common is Thingvalla, in the genitive case ; Thingvellir is the nominative, and Thingvollum the dative case.

To such as wish to travel unimpeded by the artificial shams of modern tourists, to enjoy the strange and delightful sensation of visiting old and out-of-the-way places, and of getting a look at a country and a people almost in a state of primitive civilization, I can confidently recommend Iceland. It is no place for an invalid, or those who require the comforts of hotels and palace cars ; one must be prepared to undergo exposure to cold, rain, hunger, and almost every personal discomfort ; there are no hotels, and the hospitality of the country, though great, is not suited to the dainty or the thin-skinned ; and now and then trifles must be heavily paid for. Walking is impossible except for short distances ; the roughness of the trails, the frequent icy rivers to be forded, the mudholes and the bogs and the slippery rocks would very soon tire out the most active pedestrian ; the baggage horses will stray from the path, and could not be recovered, except at their own pleasure, by any traveller on foot ; so that what comforts there are must be obtained on a horse's back.

To convey to my readers an idea of the peculiar scenery of Iceland, to see which we had traversed about four thousand miles of ocean, I think it will be best for them to mount their horses with us and join our cavalcade, enjoying in imagination what we experienced in reality, and without our discomforts, annoyances, fatigue, and expenditures.

Thanks to good friends in the capital, we were enabled to make the necessary preparations in the matter of horses, saddles, guides, packing boxes, and tent; the latter was necessary, as the crowds drawn by the king, and his own retinue, would task to the utmost the resources of the island in the way of shelter. We intended to lodge upon the cold ground, avoiding all houses and churches (the latter used for travellers) for entomological and sanitary reasons. We supplied our own stores. There are no roads for wheeled vehicles out of the city, and no wheeled vehicles in it except for heavy freight, and so the traveller must go on horseback. We were none of us graceful riders, but had seen enough of mountain travel in the Alps and California, and the Pacific Islands, to be able to adhere to a horse as long as he could carry us. The horses are very small, what we should call ponies; often weak from overwork and want of food. Consequently every person must take two horses for himself, and one for his share of the luggage, tents, provisions, &c.; or three horses to a man, one being ridden in the forenoon, the other in the afternoon,

when not in use driven along with the rest, and kept
from straying by the voices and whips of the guides.
The loading of the horses is a matter of great importance, and one which, performed in the slovenly
way practised in Iceland, gives the traveller much
anxiety, and often causes an unnecessary waste of
valuable property. Upon the frame of the pack-sad-
dle, which resembles a straddling saw-horse, are a
number of wooden pegs, sometimes iron hooks, to
which are suspended, or on which are hung, fastened
by ropes, wooden iron-bound boxes, hanging like pan-
niers on each side. In these were packed our canned
meats and other eatables, drinkables, utensils for
cooking, &c., all kept from being broken by our
blankets and small parcels placed on top. To fasten
these boxes, and many loose articles, valises, and the
like, occupied much time ; the clumsy way in which
the thing was done, the utter absence of system and
even of common sense, and the imperturbable cool-
ness with which the tying and untying were done
half a dozen times, vexed us much, and the more that
we were standing in a cold rain. After all their fuss,
the motion of the ponies invariably loosened the
ropes every hour or two, consuming much valuable
time in re-tightening, all of which might be saved by
the use of decent ropes, and such skill in tying them
as any one could acquire from a sailor in half an hour.

You might as well talk to a stone post as try to instruct one of these guides, and a sloth is about as much in a hurry as the average Icelander.

Though we arrived in advance of the king, the best horses had been reserved for him and his suite; and, though royalty pays nothing but bows, flattering words, invitations to dinner, or a bit of silver and colored ribbon, and we were ready to pay the shining rix-dollars, we had to take what was left, and pay the usual price for it.

Our guide, however, did the best he could, and off we started early Monday morning, in a drizzling rain, for Thingvalla. We were seven, with three guides and two servants (cooks), consequently our train consisted of thirty-five horses, ten of which carried our tent, food, cooking utensils, bags, guns, blankets, &c., for five days. Our saddles and bridles were poor, and the only things we had of good quality were our whips, which are essential to satisfactory locomotion in this region; our party comprised some heavy weights, which, under ordinary circumstances, would have severely galled our horses' backs; but for a saddle-cloth or blanket is substituted a thick layer of the densely rooted turf of the country, which prevents all friction of the saddle. With our rubber suits and hats we did not present a very cheerful appearance; in fact, to my eyes, our *cortège* looked more like a

5*

funeral procession than a party of pleasure. As we filed along the principal street, such a long string of horses attracted much attention, and the people saluted us respectfully as we rode along. They doubtless thought us crazy, for coming so far to see what to them appeared so common; they little dreamed that some of that dripping party were the everywhere-penetrating correspondents of American newspapers, and that others were collecting materials for books and lectures which should exhibit them in far-distant lands.

Passing the governor's house, and along the dismal road leading to the *fête* ground of the day before, the rain began to lessen, and in about two hours, as we got away from the influence of the sea, the sun came out brightly, with a temperature of 80°, and clouds of gnats which entered our ears, noses, eyes, and mouths, — not biting, but simply a nuisance from their numbers.

The country is intersected by numerous rivers, shallow, but cold and clear, which, in every case but one we easily forded, the water rarely being more than two feet deep, and often so that we could gallop right through them ; during the day we crossed not less than thirty of these streams, offering no impediment to travel, and very refreshing to our thirsty animals.

GOVERNOR'S HOUSE AT REYKJAVIK, AND ROAD TO THINGVALLA.

The first river we came to was the Lax or Salmon River, and we crossed it in fear and trembling, feeling its coldness, and ignorant of the depth of its rushing waters ; but especially afraid that our boxes would get wet, our horses swamped, and our tent immersed ; had these things happened, as the first and last, from insecure packing, might easily have occurred, we should have been in a bad plight, and the poor horse could never have carried our tent if made any heavier by water. We passed through without accident, and after that had no more misgivings, trusting to the sure-footed, tough little beasts which bore us and our baggage and provisions.

The country was barren, but yet in spots quite green, affording pasturage to many sheep ; we could see the volcanic ridges in the distance, and some shining snow-capped mountains ; the lava was all very old, covered with moss, its angles rounded by long exposure, and in this part of the island there has probably been no volcanic eruption since its occupation by the Northmen ; indeed there is no tradition in their sagas or poetic writings of any thing different from what is now seen. The ragged character of the surface, however, the marks of fusion in the lava, the fantastic and twisted shapes that it has assumed, show that once this was the scene of terrific disturbance, and the sources of the molten material are evident in

the surrounding heights. The lava does not differ
from that which I had seen in the Sandwich Islands,
nor from that of Vesuvius and other modern volcanoes. The path was sometimes indistinct, and our
spare horses gave the guides much trouble straying
among very rough boulders, where no one but an Icelander could ride ; in narrow places they would rush
together, kicking and biting, to the great prospective
damage of the packing-boxes slung on their sides, but
happily without any serious injury. The manner of
riding is peculiar in that they beat an incessant tattoo on the horses' flanks with their heels, alternately
widely separating and bringing together the legs, — a
ridiculous motion, said to have originated in the necessity of this performance to keep their feet warm, wet
as they generally are in their skin shoes ; we tried to
imitate it but without much success ; the horses seem
to expect and enjoy it ; women, astride, do the same.

We now and then came to a farm or byre, surrounded by extensive grass fields and meadows, and
presenting a cheerful, homelike appearance ; the establishment consisting of several small houses, each
with its low grass-covered roof, and each having its
special purpose. We went into several of these,
where we were hospitably received, obtaining a plenty
of milk, curds, hard bread, butter, dried fish, coffee
(and brandy, if you want it) ; but the dampness, close-

ness, darkness, and small size of the crowded rooms, made them seem very unwholesome abodes, and one is not surprised at the great mortality among children forced to live in such an atmosphere and darkness, and on such unnutritious food; the sensation was of being buried alive, on entering these almost subterranean abodes; an average tomb is more spacious, as convenient, and quite as cheerful and comfortable as some of the rooms in the poorer class of Icelandic houses.

Stopping at noon in a beautiful valley, in an amphitheatre of volcanic hills, and by the side of a clear stream, we took our lunch, and allowed our horses to graze; we threw the reins over the horses' heads on to the ground, a sign to the Icelandic pony that he must not stray; should he attempt to run, the reins getting entangled in his forefeet, soon bring him to the earth; if the reins are left on his neck, he will surely run away, or stray so far that much time will be lost in his capture. After an hour's rest we started again on fresh horses, over paths now smooth, now rugged, up and down hill, splashing through streams, picking our way along boggy places, toiling through mud, — the scenery becoming wilder and wilder, and the face of the country more desolate. The barren lava plain stretched as far as the eye could reach in every direction, a perfect stony sea, with its rude billows, dismal in the extreme from the hoary old moss which covered the blocks, — gray and silent, except from the hoarse croak of a large raven, or the shrill cry of the plover. The road had been put in such order for the king, that we were able to trot where previous travellers had to walk for hours. For guidance in the winter, when the paths along these dreary wastes are covered with snow, pyramidal heaps of stones are piled up at short distances, looking like mournful sentinels, and making good lookouts for the ravens. Late in the afternoon we came in sight of the large lake of Thingvalla, — a magnificent sheet of very deep water, at least fifteen miles long and six wide, filled with fish never caught, and frequented by ducks never shot. We knew by this that we were approaching the valley of Thingvalla, into which we must descend by the great fissure of the Almannagja, the grandest and most awful scenery in Iceland, and probably unsurpassed in beauty, which may be called diabolic, anywhere on the globe.

By this time we were pretty well tired, not being accustomed to such long and hard rides. Chilled at the start, stewed under our Mackintoshes when the sun came out, with feet wet from the splashes of the icy-cold streams, hungry and thirsty, we were very glad to know that the end of our day's work was nigh. The scenery had been depressing ; desolation, black·

ness, stillness and lifelessness seemed to carry one back in geological time, and to show him the dismal chaos before life was introduced on our planet : every thing was uncouth and primeval.

One of the striking features of this journey is the suddenness with which the weary traveller comes upon the deep chasm which admits to the valley of Thingvalla ; without warning he stands upon the brink, and sees the great plain stretching beneath his feet, one hundred feet below, green and pleasant, with a river winding through it, on its way to join the lake above mentioned.

The black precipice on which we stood was the famous " Almannagja," " the Chasm of All Men," the western wall of the valley, the corresponding eastern wall, some ten miles distant, being called the " Hraf-nagja," the " Chasm of the Ravens." This verdant plain, once the place of assembly of the " Thing," or " National Council," but, for three-fourths of a century, almost deserted, was now dotted with white tents and flags, and with crowds of men and horses, indicating the expected approach of the royal party, who were some hours behind us. It was a very lively and unexpected scene, though somewhat marred by a commencing drizzle, which added another discomfort to our cold and weary bodies. We descended by a narrow pathway, a natural shelf on the side of the shattered cliff, so steep that most of the party dismounted, to prevent being thrown by the slipping of their saddles on to the necks of the horses. Dashing through the shallow river, and up a muddy hill and narrow lane, we arrived at the forlorn-looking parsonage and church, by the side of which — permission having been asked and granted in Latin — we pitched our tent, after the usual vexatious delays attending the unloading of the ponies. As a school for patience, I would recommend to the impetuous, hurrying Yankee, a few weeks of travel in Iceland: the Icelander is rarely in a hurry, and never prompt; it seems as if they had adopted the Spanish proverb, "Never do to-day what you can put off till to-morrow."

All the available surrounding green was covered with the king's tents, and liveried servants were hurrying about, getting things ready for his arrival. We were entirely independent, having our own servants and guides, and every thing necessary for our comfort and food. Our tent was pitched near a pool of icy cold water, coming by mysterious underground passages from the distant jokuls; the cleft of a neighboring rock served admirably for a fireplace; and the neighboring parsonage fire was permitted, for the first night of our Icelandic picnic, to warm the water for our tea and coffee.

We slept well upon the ground, from the damp of

ALLMANNAGJA.

which we had ample protection, being very tired, and
the next day started, in advance of the royal party,
for the Geysers. As the principal celebration was to
be at Thingvalla in three days, I think it will give a
better idea of the country, and a more continuous
narrative of the millennial, to say what I propose of
Thingvalla now, reserving the phenomena of the geysers for another chapter.

The chasm of the Almannagja is about a mile
long, its highest point two hundred feet above the
valley ; the Ravens' Chasm, on the east, is less high.
There can be no doubt that this whole expanse, some
ten by five miles, was once, at a very remote period, a
mass of lava on a level with the top of these chasms,
the product of the streams from the Skaldbreid or
Broad Shield volcano, in full view to the north.
There are various opinions of the way in which this
valley was formed. One is, that this great plateau
of fiery lava, fifty square miles in extent, sunk either
from contraction and depression at the time of commencing solidity, or from long subsequent falling in
of the hardened crust to fill up the abyss resulting
from an earthquake or other volcanic disturbance.
Another, and perhaps a more probable one, is, that a
more recent stream of lava from the " Broad Shield "
mountain flowed over the old one, and that its weight,
with its accompanying heat, broke in and fissured the

H

cellular cavernous layer beneath, from whose interior had flowed the great mass of the old lava into the lake, leaving a comparatively thin crust above. I have seen hundreds of similar, though much smaller, depressions, formed, evidently, in some such way in the Sandwich Islands.

Be the cause what it may, this valley existed in pre-historic times, as it is described, very much as now seen, in the oldest sagas ; time and nature have in a measure covered its ugliness by a scanty vegetation. As one contemplates this lava sea, which has flowed from the ice-clad jokul of the Broad Shield, which stands in silent and snowy majesty against the northern horizon, the words of Forbes in regard to it are forcibly brought to mind. He says : " This jokul looks like some white-washed sinner, externally of spotless purity and symmetry, but at the same time the perpetrator of this matchless natural deformity, and capable of repeating it ; for in bygone ages its uncontrollable energies cleft a passage for the molten stream through the loftier ranges in its vicinity ; and subsequently, diverging, fan-like, formed the blistered field we are now traversing."

The great western precipice of lava extending for miles toward this jokul, has parallel to it for a short distance a gigantic wall, once evidently a part of the precipice, but from which it has been separated by some convulsion ; and it is by a part of this chasm, about forty feet wide, made into a kind of road by hands long since turned to dust, that you descend to Thingvalla ; it is over this precipice, too, that the Oxer River falls, meandering through the valley to the lake.

CHAPTER VIII.

THE CELEBRATION AT THINGVALLA.

FISSURED LAVA. — THE LOGBERG, OR MOUNT OF LAWS. — MEET-
INGS OF THE ALTHING. — INTRODUCTION OF CHRISTIANITY. —
THE VALLEY IN GALA DRESS. — RECEPTION OF THE KING, AND
ADDRESS OF WELCOME. — SPEECHES AT THE MOUNT. — KING
AND PEOPLE. — BREAKFAST TO THE KING. — POETIC GREETING.
— DINNER SPEECHES. — DEPARTURE OF THE KING. — DISMAL
NIGHT AND STORMY DAY. — RETURN JOURNEY. — DIFFERENT
EXPERIENCES OF TRAVELLERS, AND CONSEQUENT ESTIMATES
OF THE COUNTRY. — REPUBLICS OF ICELAND AND AMERICA
COMPARED.

> " Iceland shone, with glorious lore renowned,
> A northern light, when all was gloom around."

> " Here, as in thousand years of old,
> Sound the same words, — a voice unended, —
> As when their life and law defended
> The spearmen, with their shields of gold ;
> The same land yet the same speech giveth,
> The ancient soul of Freedom liveth,
> And hither, king. we welcome thee."

THE same force which produced Thingvalla has
fissured its bottom in all directions, rendering
it a fit scene for the important events in the history
of Iceland that have here taken place, and also the
appropriate spot for the millennial celebration. The
most remarkable and historic of these lava islands

is the Logberg, or the Mount of Laws, on which the causes of the people were tried, judgment passed, and sentence executed. This is a detached wall or island of lava, irregularly oval in shape, about three hundred and fifty feet long, and not more than fifty wide, coming down to a point so narrow that it was deemed that one stout jarl could defend it against all comers armed only with swords and spears; this is bounded on all sides, except this point, by great fissures with overhanging walls, at least fifty feet deep, where then as now may be seen a dark green, clear water, cold as ice, which comes from the distant jokuls by subterranean channels, and in a similar untraceable way flows into the lake to the south. This natural, almost inaccessible, fortress, in the middle of this dangerous and cracked old lava stream, was chosen for the meeting of the Althing, or Congress of the Nation, during the palmy days of the young and flourishing Iceland republic, — during the four centuries of its independence and remarkable intellectual vigor. When the code of laws for the government of the people was drawn up in 934 by Ulfljot, Thingvalla was selected as the place of meeting of the council for the following reasons: it was at the point of junction of the roads crossing the deserts of the interior; it was well provided with wood, forage, and water; it had been confiscated to public use, its owner having been a murderer; and it was easy of defence against ambitious and powerful chiefs. The majesty and sternness of justice had a fit resting-place amid its awful surroundings.

About the middle of the thirteenth century (1261), from the intrigues of their own chiefs and internal dissensions, the island became an appendage to Norway; from that date, with the loss of independence and the stimulus of self-government, indifference came over the people, inactivity and mental decay; when the three Scandinavian nations (Norway, Sweden, and Denmark) were united, at the union of Calmar (1397), Iceland was without resistance transferred to the crown of Denmark, to which it now belongs.

It should be remembered that Iceland was settled by high and noble Norwegians, and not by the dregs of the people; they carried there the germs of liberty and refinement, and their seclusion probably stimulated their mental powers, and made them the remarkably literary people they were, at an age when the rest of Europe was shrouded in intellectual darkness and oppressed by feudal despotism; there, in truth, the pen was mightier than the sword, and their temporal and spiritual tyrants came to dread the lampoons of Icelandic scholars more than the armies of their chiefs.

The Althing met here, in the open air, in the last half of June, in republican and colonial times, until 1690, when a house was built for it, now destroyed; in 1800, the place of meeting—though the Althing was shorn of most of its importance, and all of its independence—was transferred to Reykjavik.

Crowds came from all parts of the island, and the powerful chiefs with a large retinue, making it also an annual fair. The president was in the centre of the mount of laws, with the judges around him, seated on banks of earth; their old laws were recited, and new ones made known. The people crowded as near as the terrible chasms surrounding would permit, and to them the condemned could appeal; if their ranks opened for escape the victim was saved, otherwise his or her doom was sealed. Murderers were beheaded, witches burned by the river's side, and mothers who had killed their children were put in sacks and drowned in the pool at the base of the fall.

As the political and literary history of Iceland will be alluded to in a subsequent chapter, we will now give a description of the millennial festivities which took place while we were in this valley. Shorn of its ancient glory, though then filled with the tents of the stranger and with the crowds of a slumbering people, one could not fail to call to mind the heroic deeds of the past, and contrast them, across the apathy of centuries, with the ignoble present. The silent desert was a fit emblem of this people; a renewal of volcanic energy could alone change the one, and the rekindling of the spark of independence animate the other, — fortunately, now, there is a glimmer of the latter!

The only reminiscence of the past which I will here mention is one suggested by the volcanic phenomena everywhere thrusting themselves into notice. Here occurred that most dramatic appeal to common sense which resulted in the overthrow of paganism and the establishment of Christianity. In the year 1000 the Althing met in Thingvalla to discuss the merits of a new religion, which Olaf, the first Christian king of Norway, had determined to introduce into Iceland. The disciples of Odin and the advocates of Christianity were in the height of the angry discussion which theologic zeal always excites, when suddenly a subterranean peal of thunder reverberated around the multitude. "Hark!" cried the orator of the heathen party, "hear how angry is Odin that we should even consider the subject of a new religion; his fires will consume us, and justly." This had a great effect on the pagan side, and the chances for the adoption of Christianity had become very small, when a sharp-witted chieftain of the opposite belief, changed the current of opinion by asking the question, "With whom, then, were the

Tents at Thingvalla during the Celebration.

gods angry, when the plain upon which we stand was melted?" This was such a convincing argument, that, on the following day, Christianity was adopted by the Althing as the religion of the people, without any serious opposition.

After an interval of three days spent at the Geysers, we came back to Thingvalla, and found this valley, with its beautiful fall, shining river, and green meadows, transformed into a gala scene for the festival of the morrow. Almost every available space was crowded with tents, large and small; flags of Denmark, Norway, Sweden, Germany, France, England, and America were flying around the great pavilion; while the flag of free Iceland — a white falcon on a blue ground, the banner of the Vikings — floated from the Mount of Laws. Crowds of people were moving to and fro, and the many camp-fires, streamers, and songs indicated an important occasion. Not to obstruct the march of royalty by our republican eagerness, we drew our caravan to one side, and allowed the king's train to pass us, near the valley, — a convenience which was gracefully acknowledged by the royal party as they passed. We followed at a respectful distance, so as not to get entangled with the great number of horses. A body of farmers came about a mile to meet the king, and conduct him to the entrance of the ground. Here an address of wel-

6

come was made, the cheers and clappings from which, though doubtless pleasing to his majesty, were not well received by the ponies ; such sights and sounds were new to them ; such doings they had never experienced before. They accordingly commenced a series of jumpings and rearings, which unhorsed the governor, and caused many other laughable accidents, which must have seriously interfered with the gravity becoming such a solemn occasion. A band of young girls scattered the flowers of Iceland in the king's path, and the choir, who had taken position among the lava rocks, sung one of their beautiful national chants.

We re-camped in the old place, in a drizzling rain, which did not promise well for the morrow ; well fed, and well protected from cold and wet, we passed the night in refreshing sleep, and awoke to find a chilling wind and thick mist, which soon became a fine rain. It was a most dismal day for the principal festivity of Iceland's millennial. Forming a procession in our water-proof clothing, we looked, I fancy, like a lot of Druids, going to some sacrificial ceremony. At the mound of the flags was delivered the formal address to the king from the people of Iceland ; while full of true loyalty, it did not attempt to conceal the independent spirit of the nation, or their ardent desire for self-government, — both of which

Reception of the King at Thingvalla, Aug. 6, 1874.

had not been sufficiently considered in the new Constitution, presented by the king as the main offering of Denmark to Iceland in 1874. As showing the spirit which the people manifested, the following resolution by one of the deputies present may be introduced : —

"Whatever you do you must not flatter or speak falsely before our king. This people has done so much already to assert their right to the full enjoyment of liberty, that it would ill become us were we so little-hearted before our sovereign as not to have the honesty to tell him of our sincere love to himself, and of our determination to make the constitution, which is now demonstrably a very imperfect instrument, one by which that gift which his majesty has given to us can be made worthy of the name of a boon. His majesty shall have from us only that which we desire from him, — love from our hearts and truth from our lips ; such, it seems to me, the people of Iceland should always show to the world. It was the wont of our forefathers ; the custom is not yet so antiquated as to deserve to be given up. I am much mistaken in the king if he desires from us fine phrases rather than the plain language which conveys to him the straightforward mind of his faithful subjects."

The address began by bidding his majesty welcome to the country, and by expressing the hope that his visit might be one which coming generations would cherish. While the people of Iceland must regret,

the address went on, that his eye should rest everywhere upon the results of the government of past
ages, — poverty and misery, — it was a matter of con-
gratulation for ruler and ruled that there lingered
still, despite long troubles and severe trials, in the
heart of the nation the old manhood and endurance.
The Icelandic nation had never been so determined
as now, when the rays of the general civilization of
the world had begun to dawn upon the people by
their more free and frequent intercourse with other
countries, to assert its right to an Icelandic national
existence, the ideal purpose of which should be the
steady development of the people in every direction,
intellectual and material. The constitution contained
good seed for such a harvest, although it would require alterations in various points. A fervent prayer
for the welfare of his majesty and the royal house
wound up the address. Having listened to it when
read to him in Icelandic, the king answered in dignified tones that he gladly accepted the loyal assurances
of the people, and that he entertained the hope of
the constitution being found, when put to its practical test, to operate beneficially for the good of the
people.

At the mound were also presented congratulations
from scientific and artistic associations of Norway,
Sweden, and Denmark ; and, also, what probably was

more pleasing to the people, the poetic greeting of
America to Iceland, written by Bayard Taylor, and
translated into the native language by their first
poet ; here let me say, that, while Icelandic history
is almost unknown to us as a nation, the early events
of American discovery are known to every farmer in
Iceland.

The king then mingled with the people, in a very
friendly, yet dignified way ; but must have been disappointed, and perhaps wounded, by the sturdy, democratic, independent spirit, degenerating sometimes
into stolid disrespect, with which he was met in
public.   After this followed a breakfast to the king,
in the pavilion, given by the people, to which the
American party, with the other foreigners, were invited.   This was truly a national feast, contrasting
strongly with the one at the capital to which we
were invited, and where the eatables, drinkables, and
even the dishes had been mostly brought from Copenhagen.   But here, salmon and codfish, mutton and
native bread, formed the substantial portion of the
feast, the side dishes, and the wines, of course, being
of foreign origin.

At the door of the large pavilion was stationed a
chorus, who sang the following stanzas (Mr. Taylor's
translation being given here) in the admirable way
peculiar to the Icelanders, to the old Danish air,

"King Christian lays aside his sword," — as printed
in the "New York Tribune:" —

THE KING'S WELCOME TO THINGVALLA.

"With strong foot tread the holy ground,
Our Snow-land's king, the lofty-hearted,
Who from thy royal home hast parted,
To greet these hills that guard us round!
Our Freedom's scroll thy hand hath lent us,
The first of kings whom God has sent us,
Hail! welcome to our country's heart!

Land's-father, here the Law-Mount view!
Behold God's works in all their vastness!
Where saw'st thou Freedom's fairer fastness,
With fire-heaved ramparts, waters blue?
Here sprang the sagas of our splendor;
Here every Iceland heart is tender;
God built this altar for his flock!

Here, as in thousand years of old,
Sound the same words, — a voice unended, —
As when their life and law defended
The spearmen, with their shields of gold;
The same land yet the same speech giveth,
The ancient soul of Freedom liveth,
And hither, king, we welcome thee!

But now are past a thousand years,
As in the people's memory hoarded;
And in God's volume stand recorded
Their strifes and trials, woes and fears.
Now let the hope of better ages
Be what thy presence, king, presages;
Now let the prosperous time be sure!

Our land to thee her thanks shall yield,
A thousand years thy name be chanted ;
Here, where the Hill of Law is planted,
'Twixt fiery fount and lava field,
We pray, All-Father, our dependence,
To bless thee and thy far descendants,
And those they rule, a thousand years ! "
MATTHIAS JOCHUMSSON.

Our comrade, Erik Magnusson, a native Icelander, was the leading spirit of the occasion, and from his report to the " London Times," the following account of the breakfast, which was in reality a dinner, is taken : —

" The king and his suite, the representatives from foreign bodies, and the committee of management, had seats in the central tent. In the two adjoining, between which there was no division, so that all three formed one saloon, sat the rest of the guests and the representatives of the people, together with other men of mark.

" The first toast was that of the health of ' The King,' proposed in Danish, which was vigorously cheered by all present. Upon this the king proposed the toast of ' Iceland ' in his earnest and happy manner. Next came the toast of ' The Queen,' which was loudly applauded ; and last proposed was ' The Dynasty,' and in his speech the proposer expressed a wish that at the next thousandth anniversary it might be the good fortune of this people to have in its midst so beloved a sovereign as King Christian IX., and that he might trace the line of his descent to him on whom so many blessings were prayed for by Iceland now, and to whom many mighty ones of the world would have to look as a blessed ancestor. This toast was delivered in Icelandic, but the winding-up sentence of it was translated to his majesty by his interpreter. The king answered gracefully, expressing his high satisfaction with the sentiments expressed, and gave his royal word then and there that his son, the Crown Prince, and his grandchildren in Denmark should learn the noble tongue spoken by the Icelanders, which he sincerely regretted not to be able to speak himself. At this immense cheers greeted him.

"The hour of the king's departure now drew on rapidly. As he rode away up through the rift, nearly the whole of the assembled crowds of Thingvalla ranged themselves on both sides of the road, in order to give one more farewell cheer, whereupon he dismounted and walked through the people, shaking hands with many and bowing to all. On ascending the pass which leads out of the rift the whole of the people burst out into their last farewell cheer, which lasted until he was out of sight. It may be said with truth that Iceland never saw a more welcome guest; his dignified bearing, his ready affability, and wonderfully winning manners and unassuming simplicity, are qualities which have won for him the whole heart of the people. I heard in many places bitter complaints among the Icelanders themselves that they had not been able to give a grander reception than was actually the case. But although this no doubt stung many a proud-hearted man to the quick, yet I think he left the country with a firm conviction that to wish for a more loyal and devoted people than the Icelanders would be to wish for an impossibility."

And thus appropriately ended the ceremony at Thingvalla.

The rain at noon was falling fast, but the king's party mounted their horses, and started back to the capital, where they arrived, cold and wet, at about 8 P.M. The choir had gone in advance to the Almannagja, and sang a parting song, which reverberated grandly amid those precipices, so long unused to human rejoicings, and so soon to be again silent and desolate. After this, out-door celebration was impossible, and many songs and speeches intended for the public were confined to the small audiences within the respective tents. It was difficult for a sedate and silent people to be jolly under such depressing circumstances, and by degrees the tents became quiet, and all retired to rest, cold and damp, to wake to a morning still more wet and dismal. We started back at four in the morning, ploughing our way through the tenacious mud of the newly made roads, splashing through the puddles and streams, with an occasional miring in the bogs near the track ; we were wet through by the driving rain, chilled, and covered with mud, and the horses very much fatigued by the difficulty of the road ; it would be impossible to describe the cheerless return journey, and its utter gloom and desolation. As we approached the sea, the sun came out, and the signs

6*   I

of civilization and human occupation were very welcome ; in the bay we could see our tiny steamer, on board of which we were all safely placed about noon, and the next day we left for Scotland. We experienced, therefore, on our last day, the usual fate of Icelandic travellers, a storm of wind and rain. A steel-colored mist almost hid from view the black mountains and the leaden sky, and the wind was so furious as it swept rain-laden, over the barren wastes, that not a living being except our party was seen or heard ; now and then we could not see half a mile before us, and often not each other, and were obliged to trust to the instinct of the horses to keep the path, which, however, could almost always be traced by its muddy outline. It did not seem like earth scenery, but like the mysterious plains of the moon, barring the water, which is said not to be found on that extinguished star-satellite !

By this sudden change, I could readily explain the contradictory statements of travellers in regard to Iceland ; the one who visits this singular scenery, bright in the warm sun, and in an air so clear that the snowy mountains many leagues away can be distinctly seen, will write a very different description from the one who traverses the same ground, wet to the skin, cold and hungry, with no prospect beyond the turn in the dismal road ; the latter will be likely to pronounce Iceland a humbug, and wish he had stayed at home; while the former, as I do, will regard it as one of the most glorious countries of the world, be sorry when he is obliged to leave it, and take speedy steps to return as soon as he can. Here, as elsewhere, the scenery is in the eye of the observer, and its beauty is simply relative.

On our arrival, we had seen Thingvalla in its finest colors; we left it in its worst and most forbidding aspect. The black precipices, the green Mountain of Law, the fissured hoary lava, the sparkling waterfall, the clear river, the placid lake, and the purple mountains around, combined to make this one of the finest landscapes in Iceland; and to the people it is holy ground, around which cluster their most stirring historical associations. We looked at the Logberg as we would at Bunker Hill, as consecrated by their stern efforts for independence and justice; and an American could not fail to admire the courage of these old Norsemen, and to feel pity for their subsequent loss of liberty; and the more, as Iceland and New England are, as far as I know, the only two great republics founded on a love of civil and religious liberty, free from the sordid motive of love of gain and power.

That republic fell from internal dissensions and the intrigues and jealousies of its leaders. May we not read a lesson from its fate, profitable to our own country, where sectional strife and official corruption threaten our credit, cramp our resources, poison the fountain of justice, and bid fair to make our grand experiment of self-government a failure ; and a warning, instead of an example, for the monarchical, priest-ridden nations of the old world, who are everywhere looking to republicanism, with the United States of America as their model?

WATERFALL AT THINGVALLA.

CHURCH AND PARSONAGE AT THINGVALLA.

CHAPTER IX.

ROUTE TO THE GEYSERS.

CHURCH AND PARSONAGE OF THINGVALLA. — TREES IN ICELAND. — MILES OF DESOLATION. — RAVEN'S CHASM. — SNUFF-TAKING. — LAVA CAVERN. — MOUNT HECLA. — BRUARA OR BRIDGE RIVER. — STEAM JETS. — ACCIDENT TO ONE OF OUR PARTY. — GEYSER VALLEY. — COOKING IN THE LITTLE GEYSER. — GREAT EXPECTATIONS DISAPPOINTED. — DOMESTIC AND MEDICINAL USES OF THE WATER. — BEAUTIFUL SCENERY OF THE VALLEY.

"Everywhere is silence, desolation, monotony, — a silence, not as of death, but as of a time before life was. One is awed by the presence of the most tremendous forces of nature, — fire which has covered these peaks, and poured out these lava torrents; frost which rends the rocks and soil, and frowns down upon you from the interminable ice-ridges. Each rode alone in a sort of grave exhilaration, content with silence and the present."

BEFORE starting on the road to the Geysers and Hecla, I wish to say a few words on the church and parsonage of Thingvalla, near which we encamped for three nights.

The church is very small, as its congregation consists of the few families around the valley; built of wood, painted dark, one story high, with a little belfry; it is about 40 by 30 ft., and about twenty years old. The seats are rude and hard, and every thing of the utmost simplicity. Like other churches in the land,

it is used as a storehouse during the week, as a sleep-
ing apartment for travellers ; and, while we were
there, was filled by women, as a lodging-place more
comfortable than their tents during the rainy weather
of the celebration. It will be remembered that the
cellars of some of our old churches are still used for
the storage of cotton, tobacco, molasses, liquors, and
other commodities ; the Icelander stores his saddles
and implements in the pews themselves, removing
them outside on Sundays. Without pretence, even
uncomfortable, these little churches, seen in almost
every settlement, prove the religious character of the
people, and that worship is just as natural whether
offered in a tar-covered barn, a hut of earth, or a
stately cathedral.

The churchyards are just as unostentatious, a tomb-
stone of any description being very rare. The church
may be said almost to belong to the clergyman, and
is generally near his house. The clergy are the
most learned men of the island, and many of them
distinguished as scholars, poets, historians, and
archæologists. Their pay is so ridiculously small
that they are obliged to be farmers, shepherds, black-
smiths, or any thing else by which they can eke out a
miserable living ; and yet they are noble-hearted, hospitable, and faithful to their parishes and to strangers.
Their authority is great, and such that, in Reykjavik,

though the Roman Catholics have a chapel and one or two priests, not an Icelander has been perverted from the Lutheran faith.

The pastor at Thingvalla, Mr. Beck, was quite upset by the royal visit, but maintained a quiet dignity remarkable under the circumstances of being nearly crowded out of his home by strangers. After the king's departure I was called into the house to prescribe for a sick girl, and found the sitting-room very comfortable, — small and low-studded, for purposes of warmth, but with wainscoted walls, board floor, comfortable chairs, and the usual conveniences of a well-to-do farmer with us. The exterior was of stone, the roof covered with grassy turf, the entrance dark, damp, ill ventilated, and narrow. I stumbled on the rough, slippery pavement; hit my head against the supporting timbers, and various kinds of implements, cooking utensils, and articles of food and clothing hanging indiscriminately in the dark passage; and was quite unable to find my way alone in or out of the sloppy labyrinth. And yet, in these smoky, noisome, uncomfortable abodes live and study, happy and contented too, many excellent classical and historical scholars, whose contributions adorn the pages of the publications of the learned societies of Denmark, Norway, and Sweden.

In order to keep in advance of the king, we started

early in the morning with the same train of animals, but one less rider, our Icelandic comrade, Mr. Magnusson, having been left behind to arrange the ceremonies of the celebration. The first few miles was to the north, along the river and the Almannagja precipices, and past the fine fall of the Oxera. We then turned to the east, on to a field of rough lava, more shattered and barren than that of the day before. Here and there in holes grew some birches, about five feet high, with trunks as large as the wrist, — one of the so-called forests of Iceland: it showed what determination will do in the vegetable kingdom, for the struggle for life must have been hard, and should furnish a hint to the natives to plant trees for fuel in sheltered places. At Akureyri, in the north part of the island, is a mountain-ash, twenty-six feet high, without much foliage, the largest tree in Iceland; its branches are secured to the roof of a house in winter, its roots covered with straw, and its young shoots wrapped in wool. In the north are also small forests of birch, some of the trees being twenty feet high; these are favorite resorts for the ptarmigan grouse. Yet Iceland may truly be called a land of flowers, of an Alpine character, covering the soil where even grass will not grow. The Geyser valley, at Haukadal, is famous for its flowers, the warmth and moisture being favorable for their growth. I collected and brought home a considerable number of species. With this exception, the scene was not only utterly desolate, but positively frightful in the ruggedness and contortions of the lava; deep fissures, dislocations of great masses of rock, the plain torn literally to pieces, attested the tremendous forces which had been at work here; the earthquake and the volcano had apparently combined their utmost fury, and like demons had blasted and shivered every thing in a fiery chaos.

After two hours' ride across this plain, the snow-covered " Broad Shield" on the left, and the beautiful lake on the right, we came to a black chasm, extending from the lake to the mountains, which seemed to bar further passage; this was the " Chasm of the Raven," Hrafnagja, forming the east boundary of the Thingvalla valley, parallel to and somewhat resembling the Almannagja on the west: it is not so high, but more rugged and distorted. It is about one hundred feet deep, very much broken, the precipices overhanging and threatening to fall, the bottom filled with sharp, colossal, irregular fragments, and below these the same mysterious, treacherous, dark water; the grandeur and wildness are very imposing, and one feels like a pygmy visiting a battle-field of the Titans. This would be impassable, and would require a toilsome and dangerous circuit of many miles, had not

immense fragments happened to fall in such a way as
to form a natural bridge across the chasm, — a passage which in winter, or during a high wind or blind-
ing storm, or from the slipping or fright of a horse,
would be extremely dangerous, and at any time is
trying to ill-balanced nerves.

Though sore from the long·ride of the day before,
the cheerful sun warmed us as we passed over miles
of desolation.   The ponies behaved very well, as they
could not get out of the path without breaking their
necks.   The guides kicked their national tattoo on
their horses' sides, and enlivened the scene with some
native songs, in the intervals passing round the snuff-
horn.   I have before alluded to this disgusting national habit of snuff-taking, as exhibited in the pulpit
at Reykjavik ; it is still worse, though less conspicuous, in the common events of the day.   Every now
and then a guide would take from his pocket a small
flask or horn, pull out the stopper, throw his head
back, and pour a portion of its snuffy contents up one
or both nostrils with an air of satisfaction, indicated
by a series of suppressed snorts ; he then politely
offers it to his companions and fellow-travellers.   It
gives their voices a peculiar sound, and often disfigures
by its colored secretions what would otherwise be a
handsome face.   Now and then we came to a river
which we easily forded; we kept as much as pos-

sible on the high lands, in order to avoid the treacherous bogs, in which man and horse are often dangerously mired. Skirting one of these meadows was a high volcanic ridge, one of whose old lava streams had suddenly cooled on the top, while the fluid contents ran out at the bottom; this had left quite a cave, which we stopped to examine; it is of considerable size, and has been used as a sheep-pen for a long time. We did not go in far, dreading the vermin which congregate in such places, contenting ourselves with looking at the initials which travellers and others had cut in the hard stone; none of us felt inclined to imitate their example.

As we went around the flank of this mountain we saw in the distance a snowy range, among which was the majestic Hecla, with its complete mantle of snow (whence its name); not beautiful in outline, but grand from its size, and brilliant in the sunshine. We should soon from the Geysers have a much nearer and finer view. At about the same time we perceived at a great distance what looked like a jet of steam, and imagined we were near the plain of the Geysers; it was, however, only one of the many steam-jets with which this part of the country is filled, evincing the subterranean fiery energies which have desolated the island. We had to cross no rivers in boats, but in the afternoon of this day came to the Bruará, or

Bridge river, which would have been impassable, but
for a rude submerged and invisible bridge, — the only
river in Iceland, seen by us, which has a bridge over it.
It looked formidable, even impassable, for all we could
see was a furious torrent rushing into a deep chasm,
and in the middle what appeared like the railing of a
bridge.   The river is about a hundred and fifty feet
wide, flowing, in sheets of foam, over an irregular bed
of lava, on which the horses with difficulty found a
foothold; the two currents on each side converge in
the middle to a wide and deep fissure, into which they
dash in a rapid cataract of twenty feet in height,
with a loud roar and great emission of spray.   The
guides rode boldly in, driving the pack-horses before
them, and we followed in single file, in fear and trembling, lest a horse should fall or get frightened, when
he and his rider would surely be swept into the depths
below.   In mid-stream, the water being in some places
two feet deep, was a wooden platform-bridge, which
spanned the chasm, hidden from sight by a sheet of
foamy water; firmly pinned to the rocks, and supported beneath, it has withstood the torrent for some
years.   We passed over it, going and returning, without accident, and there is really no danger, unless the
bridge is deeply submerged, as it sometimes is: it
probably will be carried away by some sudden rise of
the river, which, with the scarcity of timber in Ice-

land, would renaer this path to the Geysers impracticable without a long *détour.*

At about 7 P.M., having been nearly all day in the saddle, weary and hungry, we came into the great, verdant plain in which are situated the famous Geysers. This, of course, excited us to hurry to witness an eruption, which we fancied was going on ; but alas ! one of our party came to grief. The paths over many of the meadows in Iceland, worn by the feet of horses for centuries, are so sunk beneath the surface, that a long-legged man, on a small horse, will strike his feet on each side, running great risk of dislocating his ankles, if the horse be going fast. The natives have a habit of raising first one leg and then the other to avoid this danger ; but Mr. Taylor, of our party, not relishing the bumps and twistings incurred in an attempt to get ahead through this labyrinth of ruts, tried suddenly to arrest his horse's speed. In the words of Mr. Halstead, who witnessed the feat, " in his excitement he drew rein as if to give pause to a steed of sixteen hands, and the small beast actually in service struck an attitude suddenly, as when a festive lamb leaps and comes down stifflegged. The horse passed from beneath his rider to the rear, and the latter coming to the front very rapidly, extended himself on his back lengthwise of the path. The pony, by a dexterous movement of his

right foreleg spared the classical features of the
rider, and prevented the destruction of the fine arches
of a well-turned physiognomy." He fortunately fell
in a soft spot, and experienced no harm other than
a few bruises and a severe shock. True to his education, the pony, whose reins had fallen over his head,
remained close by, waiting to be remounted.

In a space of a quarter of a mile by three hundred
feet are included the Great and Little Geyser, the
Strokr, and perhaps a dozen other smaller and name-
less ones ; the ground seemed honeycombed, like a
body pierced by foul ulcers, and from the pits and
mounds were issuing steam, boiling water, and liquid
mud, which made a sizzling, and a bubbling, and at
times a thumping, which indicated an ample supply
of heat and water, and suggested an unwelcome
culinary operation we should all be subjected to, if
the thin and resonant crust over this immense cal-
dron should from any cause fall in beneath our weight.
Threading our way among these ugly-looking holes,
we climbed a grassy hill, just above the Strokr, and
pitched our tent. We expected great things of the
Great Geyser, but, like other celebrities, it persistently
disappointed us. There being no time to collect wood
and perform the usual cooking operations for a party
of twelve famished persons, our cook simply plunged
some canned meats in the hot waters of the Little

Geyser, and in the same place immersed our tea and coffee-pot, and we very soon had both cooked to a T, without any expense or trouble of making a fire. The water at the surface was not boiling hot, and a finger could be plunged in, lingering not long, without scalding the skin.

Below us, in the valley, and in a more exposed and less comfortable position, were scattered the tents for the royal party, which arrived soon after us; and then this valley, usually still and lifeless, swarmed with men and horses, and echoed with the noises of expectant hundreds. We went to sleep with one eye and one ear open, but their subterranean majesties, except by a few sullen thumps, as if to exhibit their anger at the crowd of curious foreigners, made no show of their eruptive powers. We did not know when to go to bed, nor when to get up, and felt like Lord Dufferin's rooster, which, in the "high latitudes of the midnight sun," did not know when to crow, as the sun did not set and did not rise, — in fact, it was quite light at midnight, and dusky only from 1 to 2½ A.M. We slept, therefore, according to our fatigue, without reference to hours, and rose very early in the morning, the scene at which is thus described by Mr. Taylor in the "New York Tribune":—

"We took our toilet articles, and went half-dressed, to the hollow between the Geyser and the spring, where the surplus overflow is shallow and lukewarm.   It was already occupied, — a royal chamberlain was scooping up water in his hands, an admiral was dipping his tooth-brush into the stream, a Copenhagen professor was laboriously shaving himself by the aid of a looking-glass stuck in a crack of the crater, and the king, neat and fresh, as if at home, stood on the bank, and amused himself with the sight. The quality of the water is exquisite ; it is like down and velvet to the skin, soap becomes a finer substance in it, and the refreshment given to the hands and face seems to permeate the whole body."

Mr. Halstead, of our party, in one of his epistles to the Cincinnatians, thus discourses on the same scene : —

" Early yesterday morning the king sought, with a towel on his arm and a piece of soap in his fist, a place to wash, along one of the main rivulets running from the geysers ; but there were so many of his followers, who had clearly not anticipated such a disposition on his part to help himself, engaged in performing their ablutions and arranging their toilets by the stream, that he was discouraged, and retired unwashed to his tent."

In old times swimming and bathing were much practised by the Icelanders ; now they are rarely, if ever, thought of. A Yankee is much surprised to see so much warm water running to waste, when a few days' work at the Geyser streams would make any desired number of bath tubs, and with a temperature of water to suit every condition of health or disease. It is a pity to neglect such a vast national lavatory in a country where cleanliness does not rank next to godliness. If the iron horse, followed by the ingenious Yankee, ever reaches Iceland, you may expect in a few months after to read the advertisement of the "World's Great Warm Bath Establishment" at Haukadal.

The scene in this valley is very unlike what is generally represented by travellers; it is green and fertile, several miles wide, stretching in front of us to the mountains in the south-east, above which towered Hecla, silvery white, entirely covered with snow, as low as the eye could reach; behind us was a steep volcanic ridge, the geysers being in the bottom of this hill-surrounded plain; to the south could be seen the Geyser River, meandering, between its green banks, till lost in the purple haze; to the north, the icy jokuls, also dazzling white, standing like grim sentinels on the border of the mysterious desert of Iceland, — as it were, Greenland on the one side, the fiery tropics beneath our feet, and a boundless expanse of verdure on the other.

CHAPTER X.

IN THE VALLEY OF THE GEYSERS.

GEYSERS AND STEAM JETS. — THEIR WATER. — GREAT GEYSER. — ITS MOUND, BASIN, AND PIPE. — ITS ERUPTIONS — LITTLE GEYSER AND ITS USES. — THE STROKR. — ITS PROVOKED ERUPTIONS. — COOKING BY ITS WATERS. — THEORIES OF THE GEYSERS: LYELL'S, BUNSEN'S, AND TYNDALL'S. — THE POWER IN THE TUBE, AND NOT IN ANY SUBTERRANEAN CHAMBERS. — AGENCY OF STEAM. — DIAGRAMS OF GEYSER AND STROKR. — THE KING'S MEMENTO AND DEPARTURE. — FAREWELL TO THE VALLEY.

" And it bubbles and seethes, and it hisses and roars,
    As when fire is with water commixed and contending,
And the spray of its wrath to the welkin upsoars,
    And flood upon flood hurries on, never ending ;
And it never will rest, nor from travail be free,
Like a sea that is laboring the birth of a sea.

Yet at length comes a lull o'er the mighty commotion,
    And dark through the whiteness, and still through the swell,
The whirlpool cleaves downward and downward in ocean,
    A yawning abyss, like the pathway to hell ;
The stiller and darker the farther it goes,
Sucked into that smoothness the breakers repose."

GEYSERS, or spouting springs are found all over Iceland, some sending up their steam jets from the midst of perpetual ice, and others bubbling up beneath the ocean, near the coasts ; but the majority are in districts in which the volcanic agencies are

apparently dying out, this being the last manifesta-
tion of the expiring forces. Whether constant or
intermittent, they almost all deposit a silicious matter, forming the basin and the pipe, and finally clos-
ing the opening by their own incrustations.

The famous Geysers of Haukadal, which we visited, are mentioned in the old sagas, but have varied
greatly in their intensity, even within the last sixty-
five years, disturbed by earthquakes and other causes,
thus accounting for the different statements of travellers. In the middle of the seventeeth century the
eruptions seem to have occurred regularly once or
twice in twenty-four hours, but now their action is
extremely irregular.

At a distance, the jets of steam, so quiet and uniform, do not impress one with the real grandeur of
the turmoil which is going on beneath the surface.
They make less fuss than the California geysers,
whose spiteful sputterings show the utmost of their
power, while the deep and rare grumblings at Haukadal indicate the concealed but tremendous energy
within them ; it is like the snapping cur as compared
with the silent mastiff, or the caucus politician with
a Daniel Webster.

There are two kinds, one having jets of clear
water ; the other puffs of scalding vapor, coming
up through a soft mud or clay, of a reddish color,

probably from iron salts.   In the waters silica is held
in solution by salts of soda, a silicate of soda being
the principal ingredient; they are said to have great
remedial powers, externally in rheumatism, and inter-
nally in obstructions of the liver, — but, judging from
the facility with which objects are incrusted by their
silicates, it would seem as if their free use would
soon turn a person to stone; but perhaps the living
organism would so modify their reactions, as to
render their administration safe and even remedial.
One thing is certain, the water is impregnated with
sulphuretted hydrogen, as the odor plainly indicates;
this in great measure escapes as it cools, yet my
experience is that enough of the sulphur taste remains to injure the flavor of tea and toddy made
with it.

The Great Geyser seems to have always been of
about the same size; it is situated on a mound of
silicious tufa, in thin plates, easily detached and
crumbling under the feet, deposited from the overflow of its own waters; the mound is some two hundred feet in diameter, and twenty feet high, the basin
resembling a large saucer, sixty feet in diameter, and
five feet deep, in the centre of which is the pipe ten
feet across, gradually narrowing to seven, and seventy
feet deep, where it ends or takes a turn which prevents further sounding.   It is smoothly polished on

GREAT GEYSER IN ERUPTION, JULY, 1874.

the inside, but as rough as possible outside. Its eruptions, as described by all who have seen them, are preceded and accompanied by noises resembling the booming of subterranean cannon, which cause a trembling in the water and in the surrounding earth. The volume of water thrown up is immense, but not to a greater height than one hundred feet, less high than that of the Strokr, which is of much less diameter; its waters ascend, like those of a huge fountain, by spasmodic efforts, each more violent than the last, till it reaches its full elevation, assuming the form of a sheaf of silvery columns, spreading in the form of an urn or a ghostly elm-tree. The eruption rarely lasts more than ten minutes, when the force is exhausted, and the water falls with a sullen roar within its tube, leaving the basin dry, sometimes for several hours, during which periods of rest it has been often examined and measured. As we saw it, the basin was full, bubbling and seething in the centre, with occasional deep-seated detonations, leading us constantly to expect an eruption, but simply causing a slight elevation of the water in the middle, with a corresponding overflow. The surface was covered with a thick steam, sometimes so dense as to prevent seeing across the basin. This geyser is very capricious in its action, and evidently no respecter of persons; it would not spout in 1856 for prince Napoleon, nor in 1874 for our American sovereigns nor the king of Denmark, though in both these years it had displayed its strength a few hours before the arrival of the strangers.

Very near and a little below the Great Geyser is the Little Geyser, once called the Roaring Geyser, not a spouter now, its powers having been interfered with by a violent earthquake in 1789, which evidently dislocated its water-pipe at the same time that it opened the Strokr. This, often called the "Blazer," being the one in which visitors generally cook, consists of two great holes in the rock, not rising above the surface of the ground, separated by a partial partition at the upper portion, descending to a great depth; the larger division is about thirty feet in circumference, the perfectly clear water boiling gently, with an occasional overflow. The white, irregular, but smooth sides of the funnel could be traced many feet, and the singular play of ever-changing blue and green tints made it look like a fairy grotto. The transparency is such that every projection and cavity can be seen, till the eye detects nothing but the dark abyss. It is a most weird and fascinating place, and, to borrow a simile from Madame Pfeiffer, just the place to read Schiller's "Diver," where the goblet might well rest on one of the jagged points, with a monster about to rise from its blue depths.

" Below, at the foot of that precipice drear,
   Spread the gloomy and purple and pathless obscure !
A silence of Horror that slept on the ear,
   That the eye more appalled might the Horror endure !
Salamander, snake, dragon, — vast reptiles that dwell
In the deep, — coiled about the grim jaws of their hell.

Dark crawled, glided dark the unspeakable swarms,
   Clumped together in masses, misshapen and vast ;
Here clung and here bristled the fashionless forms."

But goblets of more earthy character interested us
here, as we were hungry and thirsty, and used the
lower of these beautiful caldrons for the making of
tea and the cooking of fish and canned meats. The
water at the surface was not at the boiling point, not
more than 180° F., but beneath the surface it was
sufficient for rude cooking purposes, — a very fortunate circumstance for travellers, as there is no fuel
within several miles.

The Strokr, or " Churn," is the most interesting of
the Geysers, as it may be irritated any day to show
its powers by artificial means ; viz., by pouring a cart-
load of sods down its capacious throat. This geyser
was immediately in front of our tent, and we went to
work at once to get ready the pile of sods to produce
the eruption, when we were requested not to do so,
for fear that the same dose applied on the morrow
would not operate in the presence of the king. So
we contented ourselves with looking into its mouth,

which is a rounded hole in the rock, about six feet in diameter, when we saw the water, ten or twelve feet below, boiling, with the usual bubbling and splashing of violent ebullition, and an occasional emission of steam. The whole depth is forty-four feet, and the tube is said to contract to about eight inches twenty-seven feet down.

The next morning, after his majesty's breakfast, the earth emetic was administered to the Strokr, and we all retired to a respectful distance to await its operation. After waiting fifteen or twenty minutes, during which the king and his suite mingled with the crowd in a familiar and democratic way, the internal commotion was much increased, with rumbling angry sounds; then the black mass was upheaved with violence in a column as large as the opening, consisting of innumerable jets, with whirling masses of sods: some of the streams went rolling down the hill, but most fell into the mouth, to be again ejected. The eruption lasted about ten minutes in full force, and then gradually subsided, with an occasional high jet. As near as we could judge, the height attained was not over a hundred feet; compared with that of the Great Geyser, the stream is slender and dark-colored, that of the former being more urn-shaped and pure. The eruptions will continue till the sods are discharged, or so disintegrated that they do not

ERUPTION OF STROKR, AUG. 5, 1874.

interfere with the free escape of the steam. It should be stated that the sods are a stringy kind of peat, which retain their form and substance for a considerable time.

Commodore Forbes, Royal Navy, who visited Iceland in 1859, had an experience with the Strokr, so characteristic that I will mention it. He had invited the priest and farmer at Haukadal to dinner, and he prepared it in the following novel way. He piled the customary mound of turf at the edge of the Strokr, and, taking his reserve flannel shirt, packed a breast of mutton in the body, and a grouse in each sleeve ; he then threw in the turf, and immediately after the shirt containing his dinner. After waiting forty minutes, and fearing that the Strokr had digested his mutton, he was on the point of administering another dose of turf when the eruption took place. To use his own words, " surrounded with steam and turf sods, I beheld my shirt in mid-air, arms extended, like a head- and tail-less trunk ; it fell lifeless by the brink." The mutton was done to a turn, but the grouse were in threads ; the shirt was none the worse, except in color, the dye having been scalded out of it.

Different theories have been advanced by physicists to account for these eruptions. The oldest one, which Professor Lyell seems to favor, is that water

7*

collects in subterranean chambers, which, in Iceland, must be numerous from volcanic causes, and at Haukadal, in a great elliptical plain, thirteen hundred by four hundred and fifty feet, in a north-east and south-west direction, surrounded by mountains ; this water — boiling from the elevated temperature of the heated strata shown by Professors Mallett and Hunt to exist between the cooling crust and the shrinking nucleus, whose movements are converted into heat — is forced to the surface through natural openings by the compression of steam ; and, when this steam is under an accumulated pressure, it ejects the water, as a fountain or geyser, to a height, and for a time, proportionate to this force. The periodicity is believed to be due to the varying size and depth of the receiver, and to the escape of the steam through several small outlets. As to the provoked action of the Strokr, the foreign matters put in settle to the narrow throat of the pipe, and prevent the escape of steam, till the pressure becomes sufficient to throw out the obstructions with the water and give relief.

Others, though admitting the agency of steam, do not consent to the above explanation of its action. Though it is estimated that nearly one-tenth of the island is encased in ice, and that its melting, with the frequent rains, fills the lakes, rivers, and marshes, — though much of this water undoubtedly descends by subterranean courses into heated volcanic fissures, and thence by the combined action of steam and hydrostatic pressure escapes as hot springs; and though the line of the principal ones is that of the south-west and north-east line of volcanic activity, — it is nevertheless true that they are all near the present watercourses, and that the source of their water may be from the surface supply in their vicinity. They are on different levels, even to the extent of about fifty feet; they probably do not communicate with each other, though the people believe they do; any apparent influence of one on another might depend on a derangement of the general surface supply by one in activity, without leading to the inference of direct communication. Captain Forbes, above quoted, is of opinion that the superficial waters meeting heated surfaces, owing to the geological peculiarities of the crust, both create and destroy these natural fountains.

The formation which contains the geysers is a great silicious deposit, of the variety called palagonite, three hundred and eighty feet above the sea, in which all the hot springs of the country are said to be situated; the mountain range above is a hard trachyte, but at its base, at Haukadal, are many incrustations, and one mound of considerable size, formed by these and the reddish clays of old and extinct geysers. The side of the hill above bears marks of having been perforated with boiling springs, the silicious sinter of their deposits occurring very high up ; these were gradually obliterated by their own deposits, a process now going on in the larger geysers below. The late eruption and earthquakes in the Vatna Jokul in 1875 are said to have considerably changed the character of these geysers. By the combined action of carbonic acid, sulphuretted hydrogen, and heated water on the palagonite, a bubbling thermal spring may be converted into a violent geyser, which, in the course of centuries, if not sooner destroyed by some convulsion, will gradually be filled up and become extinct. The hot spring by the above reactions separates the silica from the palagonite, and deposits it on the overflowed margin ; this incrustation, gradually increasing in height, by degrees is converted into a tube more or less deep : this, in its always-growing mound of silicious tufa, after reaching a certain height, converts it into a geyser. The long narrow tube is continually filled and replenished with a column of highly heated water, which, under the accumulated pressure of the column above, attains a much higher temperature than the original spring. The rapid generation of steam at this high temperature is the mechanical power of the geyser, which, according to the heat accumulated and the resistance of the column, throws up the stream with violence, and maintains it till the equilibrium is restored, the activity depending on the supply of water and heat, the evaporation at the surface, and weight of the atmosphere.

The water which, at the pressure of the atmosphere, might not be hot enough to cause any eruptive action of steam, at the bottom of the tube, with the additional weight of the superincumbent body of water, would acquire such an additional heat, in proportion to the pressure, that an instantaneous generation of steam would cause an eruption. The detonations so often heard are caused by the sudden condensation of the bubbles as they rise to a cooler layer of water. When the whole column begins to rise, the overflow diminishes the pressure below, and the excess of temperature above that point is immediately applied to the generation of steam ; this causes another rise and diminution of pressure and another generation of steam, till what is left is forced upward with the whole power of the high-pressure steam. The lowest part of the tube may not be interested in the eruption.

When, by successive deposits from its own waters, the tube becomes so long that the supply of heat from below and the cooling at the surface are so near equilibrium that none of the water can attain the boiling point, owing to an increased pressure, the eruptions cease, and the geyser becomes such a heated pool as

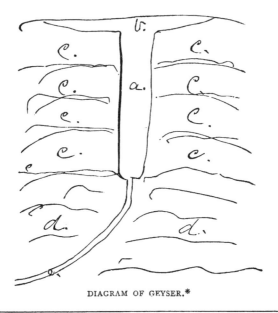

DIAGRAM OF GEYSER.*

---

* *e*, Represents a subterranean channel supplied with water from the river in the vicinity, diverted from its bed by some fault in the strata, and trying to regain its level, impelled by great hydrostatic pressure.

Finding an outlet up through the heated palagonite crust, *d, d*, it supplies the water-power in the tube, *a*, which has been built up by the successive silicious deposits, *c, c*, the lowest formed by the water which first issued from the spring.

The water enters the tube at a high temperature from its passage through the palagonite ; in the tube it is further heated by the hot silicious sides.

b, Is the shallow basin worn by the heavy fall of water in the successive eruptions.

According to this explanation, which is that of Bunsen, who visited the Geyser in 1846, the power lies wholly in the tube, and not in any imaginary and unnecessary subterranean cavern.

the so-called Little Geyser, though this received its
quietus, not from old age, but from a volcanic convulsion. It has been estimated, from the deposit of silica
made in twenty-four hours, that the Great Geyser is
about 1050 years old : in its earlier days it would be

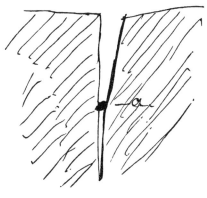

DIAGRAM OF THE STROKR.*

---

* The power of the Strokr lies also in its tube, and not in any
subterranean chamber. In the contracted portion the steam is gen-
erated, and when this orifice is closed by stones or turf, the portion
below is subjected to great heat, which it cannot communicate to the
main body ; the sudden liberation of super-heated steam, therefore,
overcomes the pressure, and causes an eruption, with the ejection of
the obstructions.

Bunsen also draws attention to the fact that water, after being
long subjected to heat, loses much of the air contained in it, has the
cohesion of its molecules much increased, and requires a higher
temperature to make it boil ; and that, when it does boil, the production of vapor is so great and instantaneous that it becomes explosive.
This, therefore, should be added to the amount of heat rendered
necessary simply from increased pressure.

quite insignificant, and would not be, and is not, mentioned in the early annals of Iceland; and it did not attract historic attention till the early part of the fourteenth century (some say seventeenth), when its tube must have been about twenty-six feet deep, not the half of its present depth. It is probably now in its stage of decay.

The geyserite, or the solid incrustations, is over eighty per cent of silica, with three per cent alumina, and a little magnesia, iron, potash, and soda.

Tyndall, in " Heat as a Mode of Motion," Lecture IV., illustrates and figures the mechanism of the geyser, substantially as just stated, and compares its stages of activity to the epochs of life. We have, in fact, the geyser in its youth as a simple thermal spring; in its manhood, as an eruptive column; in its old age, as a tranquil pool or cistern of warm water; while its death is recorded by the ruined shaft and mound, testifying to the fact of its once active existence. We find at Haukadal these four stages: 1. The little bubblers in the valley; 2. The Great Geyser, with its occasional activity; 3. The Little Geyser, or " Blazer," a tranquil well of clear hot water; and, 4. The mounds of clay and sinter behind the Great Geyser, and on the hill-side.

After waiting in vain for the eruption of the Great Geyser, the king and his party were reluctantly com-

pelled to take their departure, in order to be present
the next day at the celebration in Thingvalla. Before
going, however, he caused to be cut upon a large
lava boulder, in a conspicuous situation, a lasting
memento of his visit, in the following inscription : —

On the day of his departure a second dose of sods
was administered to the Strokr, which, after an interval so long that it was believed inoperative, finally
produced an eruption of more than usual volume,
height, and beauty ; and, just as the royal party were
turning the corner of the valley, the watery columns
shot up, bidding in appropriate floods of tears farewell
to king Christian the Ninth.

Our party started a few hours after the king, passing his train while eating their dinner in a fertile
meadow, near the sheep-cave in the side of the mountain before alluded to. We took our lunch, going
and returning, by the side of a charming stream, in
full view of the volcanic mountain, and objectionable
only from the boggy nature of the soil away from the
banks. The king repassed us near Thingvalla. Two
of our party remained behind till dark, in hope of
seeing an eruption, but got nothing but loss of sleep
and fatigue from missing their way, and a dismal ride
in a cold rain.

CHAPTER XI.

THE OLD NORSEMEN.

> " I am the God Thor,
> I am the War God,
> I am the Thunderer !
> Here, in my Northland,
> My fastness and fortress,
> Reign I for ever !
> Here, amid icebergs,
> Rule I the nations ! "

THE old Northmen, worshippers of the Scandinavian gods, would glory in the above quotation
from Longfellow's " Saga of King Olaf." The Chris-
tianized, modern Icelanders, as will be shown hereafter, are the descendants of Norwegian ancestors,
who settled the island one thousand years ago. They
were mixed, especially on the coast, with Danes and
Swedes ; all, at that remote period, much alike in language, manners, and religion, and descended from the
same old stock of the Northmen, the present inhab-

itants looking like the modern Norwegians, of whom we have large numbers in our North-western States. The characteristics of these Northmen — sea-rovers or Vikings, worshippers of Thor and Odin — were their warlike spirit, love of freedom and distant adventures, fondness for poetry, pomp, and traditionary lore, and a system of theism mingled in course of time with gross superstition. Softened and civilized by Christianity, afterward oppressed by foreign powers, who took advantage of their own dissensions, and at all times hampered by their isolation, cold climate, and barren soil, the present character of the people is a result of many discouraging surroundings.

The private life of the Northmen, at the time of the settlement of Iceland, was as different from that of their descendants in the nineteenth century, as was their patriarchal republic from the present Danish dependency. The changes in domestic life were doubtless due mainly to the more peaceful influence of Christianity.

In their pagan age, it was the custom for the father to determine, as soon as a child was born, whether it should be exposed to death, or brought up ; and this, not because the rearing of a deformed or weak child would deteriorate a race which prided itself on strength and courage, but from the inability of the parents, from poverty, to bring up their offspring.

The newly born child was laid on the ground, and there remained untouched till its fate was decided by the father, or nearest male relative; if it was to live, it was taken up and carried to the father, who, by placing it in his arms, or covering it with his cloak, made himself publicly responsible for its maintenance. It was then sprinkled with water and named; this was regarded, in pagan times, as sacred as the rite of baptism by Christians, and after its performance it was murder to expose it. Children were often brought up by foster-parents away from home, and the relation was generally one of strong mutual affection; this custom continued after the introduction of Christianity. The usual plan was either to place the infant in a covered grave and there leave it to die, or to expose it in some lonely spot, where wild animals would not be likely to find it. After the introduction of Christianity, such exposure was permitted only in cases of extreme deformity. The custom remained longer in Iceland, as the people considered it a great hardship to be prevented from exposing their children, and at the same time to be debarred from eating horse-flesh, which had hitherto been their chief means of subsistence.

I beg the reader to pardon me a slight digression here, to state that the eating of horse-flesh is one of the oriental characteristics of the Norsemen, and points to their eastern origin. In a country where the means of subsistence were limited, from warlike pursuits and the consequent neglect of agriculture and pastoral employments, the use of horse-flesh, as food, was almost a matter of necessity. It long continued in Iceland, and was abandoned only when other articles of food became more abundant. In modern days, in Europe, where the poor of large cities rarely taste fresh meat, the flesh of the horse is an esteemed, nutritious, palatable, and wholesome food. When we consider the food and habits of the horse, as compared with those of the filthy hog, we must confess that it is simply prejudice which prevents the former from being ranked in the market by the side of beef and mutton. The French have of late years been making efforts, now crowned with success, to introduce horse-flesh as an article of food. A recent French journal gives an account of a banquet given at Alfort, near Paris, for the purpose of comparing horse-flesh with beef.

The guests were distinguished men of the capital, and with the exception of the director, had never tasted horse-flesh before. To render the trial fair, beside each dish of horse was a corresponding one in beef. The animal which furnished the meat was twenty-three years of age, partly palsied in the hind limbs, and, therefore, though in other respects perfectly healthy, not likely to furnish such good eating as a younger one. "The verdict in regard to the soup was unanimously in favor of horse-flesh, tasting like beef-soup, but thicker, more gelatinous, and more capable of concentration. The banquet closed with a fine, fat fillet of horse, larded and dressed like venison ; it was triumphantly welcomed and pronounced super-excellent ; tender, juicy, high-flavored ; more delicate and melting than venison, more gamy than beef. It was by all pronounced a great addition to the pleasures of the table, — a sort of mixture between venison, hare, and beef. Every guest, on leaving, begged the cook to cut off a good slice, that he might carry it home, and let the female inmates of his house judge of its excellence." The sale of horse-meat is now regular in the cities and large towns of France and Belgium, and its price is regulated by law ; it is much cheaper and more nutritious than beef, and is rapidly winning its way to public favor. We need not, therefore, hold up our hands in horror at the old Norsemen and early inhabitants of Iceland, because they ate horse-flesh, and considered it a hardship to be forbidden to use it.

Though bodily excellence was the first object in view, mental culture was by no means neglected ; knowledge of the runes, skill in the art of poetry, acquaintance with the laws and religious and historical myths, proficiency in foreign languages and natural science, and the cultivation of eloquence, were deemed of great importance. The education of girls had especial reference to making them good housewives, and sometimes it took the direction of the study of medicine ; the mother is the natural teacher and physician of her children.

The Northmen, in their way, paid great respect to woman : hence the social intercourse between the sexes, young and old, married and single, was quite free ; and history shows, for our information, that, in proportion as woman has been the equal and co-worker with civilized man, has been the refinement and purity of social relations.

The authority of the father, however, or the natural guardians, in case of proposed marriage, was decisive, either with or against the girl's inclinations ; a widow could not be compelled to marry a second time, nor could she marry without the consent of her father, brother, or sons. Marriage was a regular business affair, and the settlement of the conditions often a shrewd bargain. If a girl married without the consent of her parents, the father could disinherit her and her children ; and the man who made her his wife, under such circumstances, was liable to be punished for abduction ; this right was not always exercised. If the father were dead, the nearest male relatives became her natural guardians. Betrothal could not be extended beyond three years, and neither party could break it without punishment and disgrace. With the introduction of Christianity, marriage became a religious rite. Plurality of wives, though not expressly forbidden, was never general, either in Norway or Iceland. Should a man lay violent hands upon his wife three times, she was at liberty to leave him, taking both dower and settlement; but such violence was rare, as it was looked upon as most unmanly. Says their old law: "Every man owes the same duty to his wife that he owes to himself;" but the husband alone possessed all rights concerning the disposal of the children. As in all well-ordered households, in all time, the husband's duty was to see to every thing out of the house, and that of the wife to have the care of every thing within it; but now and then superior, strong-minded women would so far encroach upon the husband's province as to bring him into disgrace.

Divorces were very common; mutual disinclination, the will of the husband, abuse of his wife, or the wearing by either party of garments belonging to the opposite sex, were sufficient grounds for separation. When the wife sought the divorce, she was obliged to proclaim her lawful reasons within the house, before its principal entrance, and at the public assembly. A divorce offered no impediment in the way of either party marrying again. When marriage became a religious rite, divorce was granted by the church, and never without the strongest reasons.

Their dwellings were much like those now used in Iceland, not having, like ours, under one roof several apartments of different sizes, and on several stories ; each apartment was a house in itself, and a family dwelling consisted of an assemblage of such houses, according to the rank and wealth of the owner.

The principal room was the hall or *skali*, or keeping-room, oblong in form, and generally with its long axis east and west, with the main entrance in the eastern gable ; in front was a kind of open, wide vestibule. This room was open to the roof ; the floor, of beaten earth, sometimes strewed with rushes or straw. In the middle, lengthways, was a hearth for the fire, the smoke from which filled the upper part, blackening the rafters, and escaping by a hole in the roof. Light was admitted through this hole, and through openings in lower part of roof, closed by the translucent fœtal membrane of a calf stretched on a framework of wood, opened and shut at pleasure. Glass was not in use in dwellings during pagan times, so that the houses were quite dark. Along each side of the house was a bench, — that on the north wall for the members of the family, with a high or master's seat

8

in the middle, and in front of this the sacred pillars ; opposite was a lower bench for guests or strangers, also with a high seat in the middle ; opposite the main entrance was a cross-bench for the women ; in front of the benches were footstools.

The walls were generally panelled, and ornamented with carvings, rude paintings, weapons, and sometimes with embroidered hangings. When the *skali* was for use all the year round, it was furnished with beds along the walls, behind the benches, so that each person had his bed behind his seat ; two or even more occupied one bed. Sometimes there were alcoves, or small rooms, containing beds, with costly coverings and curtains, stuffed with down, with sheets of linen or skins of the fox and other animals.

These living-rooms, or *eldaskali*, were often of very large size. One in Iceland is said to have been two hundred feet long and sixty feet wide ; another, in the same country, built of Norwegian timber, is described as two hundred and ten feet long, and twenty-eight feet high and wide : the latter is worthy of note, as the difficulty of obtaining timber from abroad, and the impossibility of getting it at home, made such structures very costly. One is mentioned in the Völsung saga, of an ancient king in Norway, which was so built that a large tree stood in the middle, the trunk of which went up through the roof, above which the top extended on all sides. In a *skali* at Haukagil, in the north of Iceland, toward the end of the tenth century, a brook ran through it. In the " Landnama-bok " it is stated in three places that *skalar* were built right across the road, so that all travellers had to pass through them, or else make a long circuitous journey to avoid them ; of course, these were for the purpose of displaying unbounded hospitality, as food was always ready for the hungry wayfarer.

The idea of this one great room or house probably arose from their ancestors, in a more genial eastern climate, living in tents like other nomadic nations ; the great *skali*, in which a large number of persons, with their domestic animals, could find shelter, came as near as possible to a tent ; the inclemency of the seasons thus did not wholly deprive them of the free-dom of motion and full supply of fresh air possible only with tent life. Their descendants have sadly degenerated from this invigorating mode of living, the houses of the modern Icelander being absolutely without pure air, very small and crowded, and almost without light.

As wealth and refinement increased, detached apartments were added to the *skali*, such as work-rooms, store-houses, kitchens, servants' quarters, bath-houses, stables, smithies, and council-houses ; and, with these, poor house-keeping, filth, darkness, and foul air. The bath-house was, in Iceland, in old times, a very important and much used addition, altogether neglected at the present day : the numerous hot springs were used to supply these bath-houses. At Reykholt may still be seen the remains of Snorre Sturleson's bath, the water of a hot spring being diverted in a stone channel into a large basin cut out of the solid rock, circular in form, surrounded by a stone seat.

These old warriors also had subterranean or earth houses, for retreats or protection, in those days when might made right, and chieftains took the law into their own hands ; these communicated by secret passages from one part of a house to another, or to some external place of escape or concealment.

The dress of the men consisted of a sark or shirt of linen or wool next the skin, care being taken to prevent its being seen : says the " Kongespeil," written about the twelfth century, " always have thy shirt cut a good piece shorter than thy tunic, for no decent man can deck himself out in flax or hemp ; " a somewhat different style from that of the residents of Manila, who wear the ornamented shirt outside of other garments, even in full dress. They also wore drawers, breeches, socks, and stockings, and shoes of skin or leather ; the upper garment was a sleeved tunic, extending to the knees, with a highly ornamented belt, and fastened at the breast by silver buckles ; gloves or mittens, an outside cape, and a hat or cap of felt, with a broad brim, completed their attire. Almost all colors were worn, but for the common dress, black, gray, brown, or white were preferred.

They were proud of their long, auburn, straight, silky hair, falling over the neck and shoulders, and confined at the forehead by bands. Great value was set by the old men on a long beard ; it is related of Thorgny, a contemporary of king Olaf, that his beard reached to his knees when he sat down, and spread over his whole chest. Men of rank always carried weapons, consisting of highly ornamented swords, spears, axes, and clubs for offence, and helmets and shields for defence. They also wore bracelets and rings of gold and silver, necklaces and chains, strings of beads of colored glass, brooches, and buckles.

The women's dress differed from that of the men in having the tunic reach to the feet, in the bodice, apron, collar, kerchief, and longer outside cape, — all more or less ornamented. Long light hair, white skin, and delicate complexion were considered then, as now, beautiful ; girls wore their hair loose, confined only around the forehead by bands of gold or silver ; if unusually long and fine, the ends were sometimes tucked under the belt. Married women and widows wore a covering on the head, that most in use resembling the high, horn-shaped *faldr* now worn in Iceland on public occasions, described and figured in the next chapter; it was usually made of white linen. They wore the same ornaments as the men, were fond of show, and tried to excel each other in the splendor of their adornments.

The chiefs were surrounded by a large body of free retainers, for service in their piratical expeditions and private quarrels, or for the mere love of display; these, skilled in the use of weapons, fearless, reckless, and obedient to the master who fed them, were always at hand for defence or offence. The various work of the household and the fields, fishing, hunting, and manufactures, was done by male and female serfs. Their serfs or slaves were generally prisoners of war, and, though having a hard lot, were protected by the laws against great cruelty on the part of the masters.

Agriculture and piracy divided the time of the old Norseman; after sowing his seed in spring, he would sail on the spring viking expedition, returning about midsummer, with his booty, to get in his crops; then he would start again on the autumn voyage, returning about the end of November, and remaining quiet all winter, planning new schemes of violence and robbery by land and sea. They had vessels of considerable size, and their seaworthiness is proved by the extent of their voyages over an ocean almost always stormy. One is mentioned in King Olaf's Saga, — the "Long Serpent," — whose keel was one hundred and forty feet in length ; it contained thirty-four rowing benches ; others had forty and even sixty such benches ; they were ornamented with the heads of serpents and dragons, somewhat resembling the Roman galleys. Though ignorant of the compass, they had such knowledge of the sun, moon, and stars, as to be able to accomplish long and dangerous voyages.

Navigation at a very early date was highly advanced, and their exploits on the ocean — whether in war, plunder, or maritime discovery — form the subjects of most of the older sagas. To this spirit of adventure was due the discovery of Greenland and America centuries before the time of Columbus.

They were also skilful horsemen, — an accomplishment in which the modern Icelanders, of both sexes, excel. Women rode, as now, sometimes astride, like men, but oftener in the chair-like saddles with rest for the feet, now in general use in the mountainous districts of Europe.

Houses being rare and far apart, travellers had to rely on private hospitality ; like the old Norseman, the Icelander of to-day prides himself on this trait. No one in need of food and shelter, be he poor or rich, could be refused admittance without disgrace to the person so refusing. In the sagas are mentioned many instances of hospitality carried to excess, as in the following cases : Geirrid, in Iceland, built her *skali* across the public road, and used to sit in the doorway and invite all travellers to come in and partake of refreshment always ready. Thorbrand, also, is said to have built so large a one that all persons passing through the valley where he lived, could enter it with horses and pack-saddles, while food was ready for every one.

Sincere in friendship, they were equally so in hatred ; and the sagas are full of the results of both.

Among their amusements, various kinds of banquets stood first, the favorite one lasting several days, and even two or three weeks, attended by both sexes. Drinking was freely indulged in, with the rioting and quarrelling always attendant thereon. During the intervals of the drinking, athletic exercises, games, songs, and recitations from the sagas were carried on. Several hundred persons often were invited to these extended banquets by the wealthy ; in one case, in Iceland, the sons of a deceased father entertained no less than twelve hundred guests. The cost of such banquets was much increased by presenting each guest on his departure a gift, sometimes of considerable value. Public subscription feasts, somewhat like the modern picnic, were quite common, and always well attended.

Athletic and military exercises were favorites with the warlike Northmen, who regarded an active and strong body, and skill in the use of weapons, as of primary importance. Wrestling, pulling ropes of hides against each other, leaping, running, swimming, walking upon the blades of oars while a boat was rowed along, and, in general, such exercises as the present Caledonians of Scotland annually exhibit to us ; the infusion of Norse blood into the north of Scotland is shown by the favorite national sports. Games with swords, archery, throwing spears and stones, fencing with axe, sword, or spear, with either or both hands, using a shield for defence, and horse-racing, were also eagerly engaged in.

Games of ball, of so rough a character that our base ball is child's play to them, dancing to songs chanted by themselves, and a burlesque on the legal customs of the country, were much in vogue in Iceland. Something resembling the gladiatorial shows of ancient Rome is alluded to in authentic sagas ; condemned criminals were compelled to fight with each other, or with bears, the only formidable wild beast available to them, being pardoned if victorious. Human sacrifices were also offered to their deities, the back of the victims being broken on the sharp

8*   L

"Stone of Thor" within the sacred enclosure of their temples.

Horse fights, playing with dice, and games resembling checkers and chess, served to pass away the idle hours of the old Norsemen, and keep them out of mischief ; they were also very fond of singing.

It was considered a sacred duty by them to respect the dead, and see that they were decently and speedily placed in a stone vault covered with earth, or barrow ; or burned, the ashes being collected in an urn. The funeral feast was a solemn occasion, at which the heir took possession of the property of the deceased ; it occurred from one to four weeks after the death.

Though the first settlers of Iceland were Norwegian vikings or pirates, they soon lost their love for such predatory pursuits, as plunderable shores were too far away, and materials for ship-building could not readily be obtained. This forced peacefulness fortunately led them to trading and to voyages of discovery, which have had a great influence on the peoples of northern Europe, and even of America. They gave up their habits of rapine, and became a law-abiding nation, with a high sense of honor, and a love for poetry, history, and eloquence unexampled in the history of the world, and a shining light amid the surrounding darkness.

According to Mr. Anderson, "the Norsemen were

the descendants of a branch of the Gothic race that, in early times, emigrated from Asia and travelled westward and northward, finally settling down in what is now the west central part of the kingdom of Norway. Their language was the old Norse, which is still preserved and spoken in Iceland, and upon it are founded the modern Norse, Danish, and Swedish languages."

The Normans, who invaded the northern part of France in 912, under Rollo, were of this race ; and his great-grandson, William the Conqueror, in 1066, at the battle of Hastings, became the master of England.

It is to the Scandinavian, therefore, and not to the Saxon, that Great Britain owes its love of freedom, courage, enterprise, and spirit of adventure ; these traits have been transplanted to America, and it is, in this sense, true that Thor, or the bold free spirit of Scandinavia, amid his icebergs, rules the nations of the North.

CHAPTER XII.

THE PEOPLE OF ICELAND.

" World-old Iceland, beloved foster-land, thou wilt be loved by thy sons as long as the ocean girds the lands, men love women, and the sun shines on the mountains."

THOUGH we might expect in Iceland the equable mildness of an insular climate, from its situation in the temperate zone and the influence of the Gulf Stream, the sea breezes are apt to drift the ice against the north shore, and produce a cold sometimes approaching that of the arctic circle. The summer and winter follow each other so closely that spring and autumn can hardly be said to exist there, — summer beginning about the last of June, and winter about the last of October. It is colder in the interior than on the coast. Changes are very sudden and very great, and the violent gales are more destructive than the cold ; a strong wind blows almost all the time, or the island would be covered with a thick ocean fog. Rains are very frequent, and the traveller must have at hand his water-proof clothing ; thunder is very uncommon.

From the names Snæland and Iceland, it is evident that the first settlers found the island with very nearly the same northern climatic character as now. With such a climate we should not expect to find any great variety of plant or animal life ; and even man has not been able entirely to resist its deteriorating influence ; his modes of life, food, houses, dress, and employments must conform to the inhospitable nature of the country.

The corn-golden hair and the azure blue eyes of the old sagas are still the prevailing type, and pink and white the natural colors of the female cheeks ; though I saw many pleasing faces, I met with none that I could call handsome. The old Scandinavian type is more manifest in the men, but their former fair proportions and physical strength are impaired by their poor food, especially during youth : the farmers seemed strongly built, with long waists and short legs ; their bronzed countenances had a dignified but good-natured expression, with a dreamy serious look, in part due to

the very prominent eye-balls. The women in the
country are pale and sallow, from the fogs and the
absence of sun-light in their houses and during
the long dark winters ; the same is true of all arctic
races of man, beast, and flower ; the sun brings out
color. According to Sir Henry Holland, the stature
of the Icelander is tall, from a greater length of spine ;
the legs are short, a fact which might be Darwinically
explained by necessity, in order to avoid hitting their
feet and wrenching their knees by striking against the
sides of the narrow, deep, rut-like paths in which they
travel on horseback ; in order to save them the trouble
of incessantly raising their legs, natural selection has
kindly shortened them ; the short-legged Icelander
has the best chance in the struggle for life. The
hair is thick, and in the women usually arranged in
graceful plaits, which are organically and not hairpin-
ically connected with the wearer's head ; their teeth
are fortunately sound and white, as the dental profession is unknown in Iceland.

From their melancholy surroundings, the country
people seem quiet, indifferent, almost Indian-like in
their stoical dispositions, patient under misery and
privation, firm and energetic in danger ; grave even
in their pleasures, they resemble their native land,
where the most destructive fires lie concealed under
the apparent calmness of the ice-clad mountains.

With little to encourage them in the present, they live upon the glories of the past, and seem like a people of the twelfth century ; though to strangers they appear sullen and indifferent, on better acquaintance they will be found frank, honest, and hospitable, the latter under circumstances requiring great self-denial. As a traveller ordinarily reaches his journey's end at night, wet from his knees down from fording the numerous rivers, it is considered a mark of true hospitality to help him off with his under-garments on his retiring to bed ; this office it was the custom of the women to perform, though it has now nearly grown out of practice. Mr. Henderson, in his travels in Iceland for the distribution of bibles, was much troubled by this custom, and his work gives the ingenious ways in which the modest missionary overcame his scruples in this direction without offending his hostess. Kissing is also very common, as a token of thanks, of salutation at parting, and in various innocent ways, at first overpowering to the modest traveller ; but he soon gets used to it, and it becomes a natural and a semi-religious ceremony, like those nowadays performed, in private and in public, in a sister State.

The emptiness of the jail at Reykjavik speaks well for their good behavior as citizens ; they are too phlegmatic and indolent to be great criminals, and the peace which goes with poverty and contentment is theirs. They cannot appreciate a joke, or play upon words.

Intemperance is said to be their besetting vice; but I saw very little of it, at a time when such indulgence would be excusable. Their alleged indisposition to work is not surprising, as they have had till recently no motive nor stimulus to labor; now, when their profitable industry can benefit themselves, instead of Denmark, there will probably be a great and sudden change in this respect.

Though they have apparently a hard lot at home, they are very fond of their native land; in a few instances some have left, impelled by desire for fame or riches, and quite a colony a few years ago emigrated to Wisconsin; but they found the yearly transition from severe cold to excessive heat unsuited to them; and they have accordingly recently taken steps to examine one of the Aleutian islands, near the coast of Alaska, where the climate and the products of the sea are much like those at home. From recently published reports, we know the constitution of the committee appointed by the Wisconsin colony to examine the Alaskan islands. This consists of Jon Olafsson, a young radical political journalist; Olaf Olafsson, a mechanic, remarkable for his knowledge of languages, obtained in his humble cottage; and Mr.

Bjornson, a sturdy, independent farmer. Should their report be favorable, a great objection would be the expense of removal to the Pacific coast ; it is hoped that the United States Government will transport them, and any others that may be induced to come ; which it could well afford to do in order to secure such an industrious and orderly settlement, which alone can properly develop the rich resources of Alaska. The Icelanders sleep in the mid-day summer heat, and work in the long light nights ; this they cannot do in the long hot summer and short dark nights of Wisconsin ; and they accordingly wish to examine our American Iceland, the coast of northern Alaska. This plan is now virtually abandoned, and the settlement will probably be in the Red River country (see a future chapter). It was reported last summer that, after their millennial celebration, large numbers would emigrate to America ; but no such intention was expressed in the parts we visited, and, from the disgrace which among them attaches to those who desert their fatherland, it is not likely that these United States will at present be so fortunate as to obtain several thousand of such hardy, intelligent, and Protestant colonists. Of the Icelanders may be said what Robert Falconer says of the Laplanders : " They live in a climate, as it were, which is their own, by natural law comply with it, and find it not altogether unfriendly. They will prefer their wastes to the rich fields of England, not merely from ignorance, but for the sake of certain blessings, among which they have been born and brought up. The blessedness of life depends far more on its interest than upon its comfort."

Estimating the population of the island at sixty thousand, which it has rarely exceeded, there would be only one and a quarter people to a square mile, or, excluding the central deserts, about seven, or one-third of the number in the most thinly inhabited of the Highland counties of Scotland. Large numbers have been swept away by pestilence and famine, — causes hereafter probably inoperative ; pulmonary and rheumatic diseases from exposure, leprosy and affections of the skin from improper food and uncleanliness in adults, and foul air and dampness in children, destroy many, or render them puny and diseased during life.

Their food consists largely of fish, of the cod family, dried in open sheds, and not salted. Nothing is wasted, — the heads are cut off and dried, and are esteemed as food ; the oil is extracted from the livers ; even the bones are used as fuel, or, boiled till they are soft, given to the cattle for food. Beside fishing, other occupations are the cutting and preparation of turf for fuel, and the making of hay, the grass being cut by a scythe about two feet long and two inches wide, the women turning it and making it into heaps. Some travellers have supposed that the tussocks or hillocks upon which the grass grows, requiring such short scythes, were made artificially, in order to increase the superficial area and increase the crop; but these, and similar longitudinal ridges, as regular as furrows, everywhere seen on the desert lava plains, are caused by the action of frost and the melting of the snow and ice in spring. They might, however, very largely and easily increase the area of their grass lands by draining the bogs, which are such impediments to travelling; this is one of the directions in which their enterprise under the new constitution may be profitably directed, and with immediate advantage to the farmers.

After this harvest comes the collection of the sheep from the summer fields for winter protection and feeding; instead of shearing, they pull off the wool, or even allow it to fall off spontaneously; the first might seem a cruel process, but it is not so, as the wool remains till it is loose, and the long coarse hair, the chief protection from the cold rains, is thus preserved.

The days of the week are not like ours, with the exception of Sunday and Monday; the other names were changed by a Romish bishop, because he thought

they were too suggestive of heathenism, recalling Tir
the northern Mars, Odin, Thor, Frigg, and Saturn.
The Iceland names correspond to third day, mid-week
day (German Mittwoche), and fast day, Saturday being
washing day, as it was the universal custom to take a
bath on that day. Time is not reckoned by the hour
of the day, clocks and watches in many places being
unknown ; but the day is divided, according to the
position of the sun in the heavens, into eight periods
of three hours each, called respectively, beginning at
9 A.M., which is day, noon, evening, mid-evening,
night, midnight, morning, and mid-morning, the last
being 6 A.M., at which they generally rise ; they remain up till late in the evening, a custom due to the
light nights.

They have an ingenious way of ascertaining whether
a month has thirty or thirty-one days : shut the fist ;
let the first knuckle represent January, with thirty-
one days, and the depression between that and the
next, February, with its lesser number ; thus every
month which corresponds to a knuckle will have
thirty-one days, and every one corresponding to a
depression thirty days or less ; the little-finger knuckle
represents July, and, beginning again with the fore-
finger, that knuckle stands for August, and so to
December. This is taken from Bishop Arneson's
finger rhymes for calculating time.

In midsummer the women make up parties to go into the borders of the interior desert in search of the Iceland moss, a nutritious lichen used as food, and by other nations as a demulcent in pulmonary diseases ; taking their tents and provisions, and men enough to protect them from the robbers believed to inhabit these regions, it amounts to a sort of picnic, of several weeks' duration, and is looked forward to as the great excursion of the year.

The old Norsemen brought with them from Norway a style of architecture in some respects well adapted to a cold climate. Each apartment formed a house by itself, with its small closets, narrow passages, and a loft ; and many of these houses, placed close together, constituted a dwelling. There being no native timber in Iceland, their dwellings were made of lava, earth, and turf ; the floor of stone or firmly beaten earth ; in the centre, or in one corner, was a stone fire-place, the smoke, when it went out at all, passing through a hole in the roof, covering all the upper part of the room with soot; this opening also served to let in light, in the absence of windows, which would let in the cold.

The modern Icelanders have not much improved on the old type, as a house now consists of a conglomeration of small buildings, in all some fifty feet long and twenty-five or thirty deep. The dwelling-house

proper is in the centre, flanked on each side by cow-
sheds, smithy, and the various outhouses; the turf
and lava walls two to three feet thick ; the gable-roof
is boarded, covered by a thick layer of grassy turf,
and surmounted by a weather-cock. The entrance
of such farm-houses as we saw in the interior (the
city houses being modern in style and conveniences)
was by a long, dark, narrow, ill-ventilated passage,
with stone floor, uneven, muddy, and wet, rough sides,
and so low that you bump your head at every step
until you learn to bend your body almost double;
this leads through the house to the kitchen, where
the fire of peat or dung or bones or wood is kept up;
this is the only fire in the house, no matter how cold
the weather may be, and you can imagine that the
atmosphere from fuel and occupants is not of the
purest ; and, in fact, to our senses quite unendurable.
Fortunately, their sense of smell is deadened by the
national habit of snuff-taking ; whether the women
indulge in this I cannot say, but it is probable that
with age femininity loses its characteristic love of
good looks with them, as with us, and that certain
masculine habits, in the direction of tobacco, are
allowed to disfigure the female countenance, which
then assumes that of man.   The irregular dwelling-
rooms open on each side, in which scythes and saddles, cod's heads and cradles, nets and spinning-wheels,

wet clothes and musty meat, and the innumerable articles of house-keeping, husbandry, and clothing, are mingled on floor and wall in dire confusion; in fact, a tidy housekeeper would go crazy here in half an hour. Downstairs, and in the lofts, are ranges of boxes or bunks, separated only by a head-board, filled with feathers, sea-weed, or hay, and covered with old clothes, worn blankets, and musty skins. A whole family usually sleep in one room, for warmth, and two or three in a bunk is the common order of things in a large family. No air can get in unless through cracks in walls, doors, and windows, and the idea of the necessity, or even the desirability, of fresh air never enters their heads. One may well believe the assurances of travellers that their poorer houses and their persons are infested with vermin; as we slept on the ground, away from all houses, under our tent, we were entirely free from these annoyances; we did not even enjoy the hospitality of a church, whose sacred precincts these degraded dipterous insects do not scruple to enter and occupy. Sometimes openings are found in these close rooms, carefully closed by corks, which at the earnest solicitation of a suffocating traveller are removed for a minute or two, and closed as soon as the cold air is felt. Though their houses were rudely furnished, and not overclean, they were totally unlike the uncomfortable cabins and

shanties of our poorer classes in and near large
cities ; there were no signs of destitution, and, though
homely, they were sufficient for their simple wants.

A national costume is worn only by the women,
who always adhere to old customs longer than men,
being naturally more conservative. The men dress
very much like laboring and seafaring men in the
northern ports of Europe; their clothes being made
of homespun wool, thick and serviceable ; the shoes
are made of skin, which is easily wet through, giving
a dirty appearance and bad odor, and from their cold
dampness must be very unhealthy. As there are, it
is said, very few shoemakers in Iceland, and no tailor,
those who do not dress in the costume of the country,
must import their clothes and shoes.

The every-day dress of the women is simple, neat,
well-fitting, with long sleeves and apron, warm and
serviceable, and of woollen material. On ordinary
occasions all dress alike, so that it is not easy to tell
the class in society to which an Icelandic woman belongs ; in high life and in ceremonious calls, Paris
styles are followed here as everywhere. The every-
day head-dress is the *hufa*, a coquettish, flat disk of
black woollen cloth, like that worn by the Greek
women, fastened on the top of the head by pins,
having a long tassel of black silk, ornamented with
silver or gold, falling over one ear ; this is worn by

NORSEMAN FROM FAROES.

STUDENT'S DRESS.

FESTIVAL COSTUME.
The Faldr.

COMMON HEAD-DRESS.
The Húfa.

young and old, married and single, and is very becoming. On any national or public festival, the
women adopt the picturesque costume so well seen
during the visit of the king. The most characteristic feature is a kind of helmet (*faldr*), a high,
white muslin, or fine linen head-dress, fitting closely
on the forehead, and loosely behind, about a foot
high, and gracefully curving forward ; the edge is
embroidered with gold cord and stars, the top enveloped in a veil of white tulle, worn very artistically,
and hanging far down the back.

The close-fitting bodice, usually of dark cloth, is
richly embroidered, with gold and silver leaves around
the neck, in front and on the edges, and laced with
silver chains ; the shoulders, sleeves, and wrists are
similarly ornamented. They wear beside elaborately
worked jointed silver belts, filigree buttons, large
hooks and eyes, and immense brooches and bunches
of ornaments, of strange patterns, made upon the
island ; they are sometimes inlaid with precious
stones, are generally heirlooms in the family, and
indicate the position and wealth of the wearer.

The early history of Iceland, according to the Irish
monk Dicuilus, who wrote a geography in 825, would
comprise the introduction of Christianity by priests
of that nation in 795 ; and some names and a few
relics found go to show the truth of this statement.

9   M

But, whatever progress the Romish religion had made among the Celtic people who had colonized Iceland at that remote age, the advent of the Norsemen in the next century utterly obliterated it and its believers, and the Scandinavian deities held sway over the minds of the new settlers till the reintroduction of the same form of theology toward the close of the tenth century was inaugurated by the efforts of king Olaf.

The introduction of Christianity in the year 1000 at Thingvalla has been alluded to in a former chapter; the heathen party were conciliated by permission to continue to expose their children, eat horse-flesh, and worship the old gods in private; the northern and eastern people refusing to be baptized in *cold* water, were afterward admitted to the church at more comfortable *warm* springs. Their improved knowledge and increasing disbelief in the old deities had prepared the way for the new religion, which required only toleration to obtain an easy victory over the old one; from this time, with the abolition of the superstitions and customs of the worship of Odin and Thor, began a new era for Iceland, during which, for more than three centuries, and until the loss of their inde pendence, it attained its highest intellectual and polit ical development, — its golden age.

Like other Scandinavian nations, they at first be-

lieved in the simple but grand doctrines of one good
and supreme God, the immortality of the soul, and a
future state of retribution according to the eternal
laws of morality and justice; but, as in subsequent
systems of theology, human weakness, passions, and
priestcraft disguised these simple truths under a complicated and doctrinal covering of mythology, deifying
some of the powers of nature, both good and evil,
and thus so alienating and disgusting the minds of
its votaries, that they were ready for any change
which promised greater freedom of thought and
action. Thus was the way prepared for a Romish
system, which, for the same reasons, a few centuries
later, gave place to Protestantism ; and, from the
signs of the times, it would now appear that this last,
overgrown by the same deforming excrescences, is
called upon by protesters within its ranks to cleanse
itself from the rust of ages, and to return to the simplicity and purity of its founders. We can no more
conceive how strong minds could receive as truths
the absurdities of the tenth century, than we can now
reconcile with the intelligence of the nineteenth century certain Romish and Protestant dogmas which
command an unthinking or an interested assent.

Though colonized by Norwegian vikings, Iceland,
from its isolated situation, did not continue a nation
of robbers, but was soon the country of law-abiding

citizens, lovers of justice and honor, peaceful discoverers and traders, and cultivators of poetry, history,
and eloquence. Their refined civilization was indicated by the respect paid to woman and her kind
treatment ; though prisoners of war were treated as
slaves, polygamy was very rare. Poverty, resulting
from idleness or crime, was punished as a political
offence, by deprivation, in case of parents, of the
rights of citizenship, and of children, of the rights of
inheritance ; this was rendered necessary in a country
where the means of subsistence were so scanty.
When poverty was the result of misfortune, disease,
or old age, each parish, or the relatives, were obliged
to make provision for relief.

Christianity softened the rude manners of the
people, and by degrees the ordeal by single combat
gave way to law and justice, the exposure of children
ceased, and the eating of horse-flesh, brought from
the East and a part of the religion of Odin, was generally abandoned.

Authors have alluded to their probable descent
from oriental forefathers, and are constantly reminded
in Iceland of the East ; the people from the earliest
period were dwellers in tents, and their government
was patriarchal ; like Arabs, they regard as sacred the
rites of hospitality ; their long caravans of horses,
crossing the deserts, salute each other with a courtesy

peculiar to the worshippers of the sun. Other oriental characters are their fondness for the horse and
their aversion to walking; the use of milk curds as
food for themselves, and of dried fish for their cattle,
and of dried dung for fuel; and especially their love
of listening to stories of the exploits of their ancestors. It is remarkable to trace these evidences of
distant wanderings in such different climes. In the
twelfth century monks and convents were numerous,
and the country contributed its share of men and
money to carry on the Crusades and other projects of
the papacy.

As in other parts of Europe, early in the sixteenth
century, many of the Romish clergy were a disgrace
to their profession, and the purity of their religion
had degenerated into those outward rites, heartless
observances, and dogmatic articles of faith, which,
taking the place of morality, show that a system of
theology has reached its period of decay, when returning reason and increased intelligence demand a ref-
ormation. The doctrines of Luther between 1540 and
1552 were generally adopted in Iceland, under king
Christian Third of Denmark, and in 1558 the last trace
of popery was abolished by the suppression of the
monasteries, of which there were nine on the island;
they have remained strict Lutherans ever since, with
the advance in morals, civilization, and freedom, which

accompanied this change in other parts of Europe. Many relics of the Romish faith are still to be found in the island. The Vatican, however, was so far off, that the Icelandic priests did not hear the pontifical thunder ; and so far obeyed the laws of nature and common sense, repressed by this church nominally in this direction, as to marry like other people ; in some other respects they were very independent.

There are about ninety parishes in Iceland, whose pastors receive what to our clergymen would be considered a ridiculously small salary, from $150 to $200 a year, eked out by the hard-earned but willing contributions of their small flocks. It is difficult to persuade one's self that the fashionable frequenters of the luxurious temples of the Fifth Avenue and the " Back Bay " are worshippers of the same lowly Jesus as the humble Lutherans in the plain box-like churches of Iceland ; or that the occupants of such different pulpits are laborers in the vineyard of the same Lord.

Going to church is for the Icelanders almost their only opportunity for social intercourse ; before and after the services occur those little interchanges of kind words and good-will, which the paucity and scattered positions of the population would otherwise render impossible.

To show the absurdity of making religion in any

way consist of what one eats and drinks, or of laboring in the obtaining and preparing of the food of
nations, an industry of Iceland, and certain facts in
natural history, may here be mentioned.

A principal occupation of the Lutheran Icelanders is fishing for cod and allied species, which they
prepare and export chiefly for the markets of the
Catholic countries of southern Europe, one of whose
sacred duties, by authority of an infallible head of
their church, is to abstain from meat on Fridays;
French and other fishermen do the same; to this
Romish custom, which the people of the north disbe-
lieve in, much of their prosperity is due. The smaller
whales, dolphins, and porpoises are also hunted in
these waters, and their flesh used for the same purpose; papal infallibity has for centuries declared that
the last-named creatures are fish, and may therefore
be eaten, when meat is forbidden, and a deadly sin
thus escaped; what a shock it must have been to the
chief priests when natural history proved that cetaceans, or whale-like animals, though living in the
water and shaped for rapid progression in it, are true
warm-blooded mammals, breathing air by lungs and
not by gills, bringing forth their single young alive
and nourishing them with milk, in no way resembling
the cold-blooded, scaly fish, except in shape and the
element they live in. Whatever the amount of sin

there may be (and all Protestants and some Catholics think there is none) in eating meat on prohibited days, is equally incurred by the partakers of the fish-like cetaceans ; the flesh of the latter, which in theologic ignorance is permitted, is just as much meat as beef, pork, or mutton. Such religion as that may well dread the dissemination of knowledge, and insist upon denominational schools in which the wax of the youthful mind may be made to assume the never-changing form of sectarian bigotry.

When we consider the inclemency of the climate of Iceland, the scanty means of subsistence, the ravages of ice, fire, and water which they have to contend with, in addition to the terrible epidemics to which they have many times been subjected, with their chronic and till recently almost hopeless political and commercial depression, it seems very remarkable that the Icelanders should be the hospitable, disinterested, honest, liberty-loving people which the testimony of all travellers among them uniformly asserts.

CHAPTER XIII.

POLITICAL HISTORY OF ICELAND.

PECULIAR HISTORY. — BRITISH AND NORWEGIAN SETTLERS. — NADDODR AND GARDAR. — FLOKI, OF THE RAVENS. — INGOLF AND LEIF, A.D. 874. — NORWEGIAN EXODUS. — REPUBLIC OF ICELAND. — MAGISTRATES AND THEIR DUTIES. — INTRIGUES OF NORWAY, AND DOWNFALL OF THE REPUBLIC. — DECLINE OF THE PEOPLE. — LATER HISTORY. — REVOLUTIONARY DISTURB-ANCES. — GOVERNORS OF ICELAND.

> " What should we do, but sing his praise,
>   That led us through the watery maze
>   Unto an isle so long unknown,
>   And yet far kinder than our own,
>   To land us on a grassy stage,
>   Safe from the storm and tyrants' rage ? "

THE political, literary, and religious history of Iceland are so interwoven that it is difficult to treat of them in separate chapters ; but, at the risk of slight repetition, I shall endeavor in this to confine myself to the first, reserving for the next a brief account of the maritime discoveries which connect America with the Old World.

We should not expect to find on a lonely island in the Northern Ocean — a land with little agricultural or mineral wealth, with a bleak climate, and apparently

9*

almost uninhabitable — such a history as that of Iceland, interesting in a moral, historical, political, and ethnological point of view. We see man here struggling
for existence under the most adverse circumstances,
and yet early developing a literature, civilization, and
religion, and cultivating the principles of liberty and
self-government, when more favored nations were in
their days of darkest ignorance and superstition.

The generally received opinion that the first, or at
least the principal, actual colonization of Iceland was
by Norwegian refugees in the ninth century has been
denied by good authority. Ireland and the British
Isles sent many colonists to the Shetlands, Faroes,
and Iceland long before the time of Harald the Fair-
haired ; at that time and afterward many such colonists arrived, according to their own " Landnamabok,"
who were Christians, and called " Papas," supposed to
mean priests. Professor Munch, of Norway, and Mr.
Dasent are of the opinion that as many came from
the western isles as from Norway ; however this may
be, the Scandinavian wave overwhelmed them, and
the Norse element has since prevailed.

Colonized, then, by the hardy Norsemen who left
Norway to enjoy civil liberty, the annals of Iceland
are not those of the bloody wars which then prevailed
in the rest of Europe, but those of maritime adventure and discovery ; of man's contest with the agen-

cies of fire, ice, and water ; and of a literary culture which challenges our admiration.

With a small and necessarily scattered population, whose intercourse with each other was impeded by deserts, lava streams, icy mountains, and furious rivers ; decimated by famine and pestilence; their means of subsistence destroyed by the earthquake, volcano, and glacier, — the history of Iceland is the most remarkable during the dark ages, as showing how literature and religion can elevate humanity, under circumstances which, without these, invariably lead to degradation.

Without discussing the unprofitable question whether Iceland was the Thule of the Greek geographers (which it probably was not), we may pass to its colonization by the Norwegians toward the end of the ninth century. These Norsemen, or Vikings, were of necessity bold mariners, and, it must be confessed, nothing less than freebooters, who, with their vessels, despoiled France and Great Britain, where they took permanent possession of the Shetland and Faroe Islands, as stated in previous chapters.

In 861, one Naddodr, driven from his course by a tempest when returning to Norway from the Faroes, came upon the east coast of Iceland, the Reidar fiord ; not liking the looks of the shore, he sailed away in a thick snow-storm, calling the country, for that reason, Snæland. Gardar, a Swede, sailing from Denmark to the Hebrides, was driven by a storm, in 864, also to the east coast of Iceland, whence he sailed to the north coast, spending the winter at Husavik; he returned home the next year, giving a favorable account of the island, calling it Gardarsholm. In the following year, or in 865, Floki, another Norwegian pirate, set out to explore this island. The compass being then unknown, after he had touched at the Shetlands and the Faroes, and when at a good distance from the latter, where he obtained three ravens, he allowed one to go free; the bird directed its course to the Faroes, the nearest land; sailing on, he let loose another, which, after rising to a great height, and seeing no land, returned to the vessel; a few days after, he freed the third bird, which flew to the North, where Floki followed it, touching at the east coast of Iceland, whence he sailed south and west, landing at a fiord on the north-west coast, where he spent the winter. He abandoned this part of the island, calling it Iceland, from the great quantity of drift ice in the northern bays (Vatn's fiord); he passed a second winter at Hafna fiord, just south of Reykjavik, returning to Norway the next spring.

The course taken by these mariners was a very indirect one, unnecessarily long by about five hundred miles, by way of the Shetlands and Faroes, the distance from Norway to Iceland being somewhat over six hundred miles ; and, when we consider the ships of that period, and the rough seas of these northern latitudes, we must admire the courage, perseverance, and endurance of these hardy voyagers. They make no mention of inhabitants, though the Norwegian colonists, who went a few years after, discovered traces of former visitors in fragments of books, and religious implements, probably those of Irish Catholics. It is believed that Irish Picts visited and colonized Iceland in the eighth century, and traces of such occupation are found in several of the geographical names of the fiords ; their books, bells, and crosiers were left behind, as "they chose not to live with the heathens." But this occupation had no influence upon the future of the island, and is of no historical importance as far as the progress of civilization is concerned.

In 870, Ingolf and Leif, cousins, obliged to leave Norway on account of a bloody family quarrel, explored Iceland, which name the island retained after the visit of Floki ; and, after spending a winter on it, returned, satisfied that it was better than their old home. In 874, they set sail again for Iceland, with their families and friends, and thus and then laid the foundation of the Icelandic nation, whose millennial anniversary was celebrated, in our presence, in August, 1874.

Ingolf carried with him the sacred pillars of his house, which he threw into the sea on approaching the land, determined to fix his habitation where they were cast ashore ; but, being separated from them by a sudden storm, he was obliged to land on the south-east coast, at a place hence to this day called Ingolfs-hofde, where he dwelt three years. Having then heard that the pillars of his house had been cast upon a beach on the south-west coast, he removed to the place, where he founded Reykjavik, the present capital. His cousin, Leif, was murdered by his Irish slaves, on account of his cruel treatment of them ; they then fled to the Westmann Islands, where Ingolf pursued and slew them.

After Harald the Fair-haired in 872 had defeated the Norwegian chiefs who had rebelled against his arbitrary decrees, the best and bravest of them took refuge in Iceland, which they well knew had been settled by their adventurous countrymen. For more than sixty years, the chiefs and their families and re-tainers flocked to Iceland, until the cause for emigra-tion ceased and the best lands had been occupied.

Settled in the true spirit of liberty and justice, the only foundations for a republic, they lived under a patriarchal government, each man under his own chief, as long as there was land enough to be occupied; but some greedy chiefs had in the beginning taken more than they could use, and the colonists began to interfere with each other. Amicable settlements soon became impossible, and their fiery spirits had recourse to the sharp decision of the sword, which was often very unjust; so that they early perceived the necessity of a common government, general laws, and courts of justice. They adopted their native Norwegian Althing, or regular assembly, which instituted a code of laws in 928 at Thingvalla, to which the meetings had been removed from the south part of the island. This assembly met in the last half of June, and continued about three weeks; every freeholder esteemed it a privilege to attend and express his opinion on matters of general interest, — a right precious to all Scandinavian peoples.

In the words of Mr. Brace, among them was found " the respect for law which has characterized every branch of the Teutonic race since; here, and not in the Swiss cantons, is the beginning of Parliament and Congress ; here, and not with the Anglo-Saxons, is the foundation of trial by jury; and here, among their most ungoverned wassail, is that high reverence for woman, which has again come forth by inheritance among the Anglo-Norse Americans. The ancestors (at least morally) of Raleigh and Nelson and Kane and Farragut appear among these sea-rovers."

The physical configuration of Iceland, and the difficulty of maintaining large bodies of men at one locality, rendered war impossible, unless the feuds of the chiefs deserved that name ; fighting with the savage nature around them demanded most of their energy ; the history, therefore, of this people is quite different from that of the other nations of Europe. The government was at first patriarchal, and they naturally adopted the "thing" or council, to which they had been accustomed in their native land of Norway. When the code of laws prepared by Ulfljot was accepted by the people, the island was divided into four chief parts, each of which was subdivided into three (the northern into four), in each of the latter there being three principal temples or hoffs ; these thirds were again subdivided into smaller sections or *hrepps*, usually ten, corresponding nearly to the parishes as now defined. Each of these divisions had its magistrates, in the election of which the people had a voice. The lowest magistrates, five of whom were chosen by the people in each division, were required to be men of wisdom and high character, and generally possessed of considerable property; they administered justice, looked after public morals, and had the care of the poor in their respective districts.

The magistrates of the main divisions or provinces were the judges and priests of their districts, presiding in the assemblies and the temples; they were called *godar*, or *hofgodar*, and their office was hereditary, constituting a kind of aristocracy, which afterward led to serious troubles; the income was small, and the influence exerted was, at first, little else than personal; the powerful chiefs often exercised more authority than the prefect of the province. Meetings of the people were held at least once a year in the principal temples, the people being summoned to attend by sending round a wooden mallet named Thor's hammer, after the manner of the fiery signal in the Highlands of Scotland. Ordinary disputes were settled at these meetings by a trial with judges, juries, and witnesses, and then, as now, the influence of friends was often more powerful than truth and justice; human law never was, and probably never will be, equity.

The highest officer was the *lagmann*, the supreme judge of the island, and president of the Althing. He, with other chiefs, made the laws, and saw that they were enforced; at first, chosen for life by the assembly, his term of office was afterward limited; during the three hundred and thirty-two years of the

N

existence of the republic, thirty-one persons held this office, and seven of these were *twice* chosen ; there is no record of a *third* term.

The Norwegian kings had long been jealous of the republic of Iceland, and were always intriguing to obtain a controlling influence in its councils. This they began conspicuously with the introduction of Christianity, attempting to combine the temporal with the spiritual power, attended with the intrigues always springing from such incompatible union, whether in the eleventh or the nineteenth century. King Harald Hardrade, and his half-brother Olaf, were active in this direction, but without much suc- cess against the liberty of Iceland, whose clergy were so independent of the Vatican, that they continued to marry, like other citizens, till the loss of their country's freedom.

As the power and wealth of the chiefs increased, those of the people diminished ; might overruled right ; reverence for the laws became less and less ; the government fell into the hands of an ambitious oli- garchy ; and in the middle of the thirteenth century, amid the fierce battles of the most powerful leaders, the republic of Iceland came to a violent end, and largely through the agency of the high chief, Snorre, whose treachery is hardly atoned for by the fame he brought his country by his poetical and historical works. This man — the Cicero of Iceland — died by the hands of assassins, led by his own son-in-law, in September, 1241.

In 1262–64, under Hakon VI., king of Norway, the people took the oath of allegiance to him, but with the express understanding that the country should retain its independence, and be governed by its own laws. It was never, therefore, completely incorporated with Norway, nor afterward with Denmark. They have always been a partially independent and isolated people, and for this reason preserved their ancient language in all its purity, of which they are to this day extremely proud.

It was in the independent but turbulent age of Iceland, for about three centuries, that were composed the poetical and historical works, hereafter alluded to, whose glory yet sheds a light over the land. With its allegiance to Norway, the history of Iceland may, in great measure, be said to end; for, though nominally independent, it was in reality little more than a province of that kingdom, and afterward, in 1380, of Denmark. No longer self-governed, the people lost their political vigor and mental power; the lively interest in public affairs gave place to apathy and trust in the foreign state; literature declined, as the skald had neither the inducement nor the materials for his verses; wealth diminished, and commerce fell into the hands of foreigners ; the Scandinavian language, kept pure in Iceland by its isolation, became so corrupted in Norway, Sweden, and Denmark by German intermixture, that the native poet found himself in those countries speaking an unknown tongue.

Much of the history of their fourteenth century is an account of the earthquakes, volcanic eruptions, and pestilences which ravaged the island, sweeping off nearly two-thirds of the people, and impoverishing the remainder. It is probable, as before remarked, that British fishermen landed on the shores of Iceland before its discovery by the Norwegians, and their commerce was not interrupted by the new settlers. During the fifteenth century, the trade in dried fish was quite extensive, and, in the sixteenth, so great, and the relations between Denmark and Great Britain so intimate, that Christian the Second came very near pledging Iceland for a sum of money ; how this event might have changed the destiny of the island it would be unprofitable now to speculate. The English fishermen went there in large numbers, till oppressive regulations drove them away in 1782. Had the Danish monopolists not interfered, this com merce would have been of great advantage to all concerned ; but the prohibitions were so strict that the Icelanders would have starved to death, had not English merchants supplied them, at great risk, with articles necessary to life.

The seventeenth century was remarkable for the oppression of these helpless islanders by French, English, and Algerine corsairs, who plundered their coasts, murdered their people, and carried off many into captivity.

In the eighteenth century the small-pox destroyed about one-third of the population; terrible famines swept off vast numbers, and volcanic eruptions of unusual severity prevailed.

In the beginning of the present century the last link which bound them to the memory of their old independence was broken, and the Althing, which for nearly nine hundred years had met at Thingvalla, was transferred to the capital; even the formal meeting in the old place, though without any political significance, amid the rocks and precipices so sacred to liberty, was enough to show them that they had a national existence. When that meeting ceased, the spirit of the nation fell — let us hope, not for ever.

Iceland has suffered much from fatal epidemics. While some contagious diseases were imported, others arose from volcanic emanations and from lack of proper food; but many also were due to the absence of ventilation and of light, the people, as a rule, living in very foul air and in damp houses. Indeed, it is a mystery how children can be raised with such surroundings, which are more fatal, and none the less reprehensible, than the exposure of the innocents by the ancient Norsemen.

In the early part of the nineteenth century, when the northern nations of Europe were involved in war, Iceland suffered to such a degree from want of the necessaries of life, cut off from Denmark, that Great Britain allowed supplies to be carried to Iceland and the Faroes, from motives of humanity; though nominally enemies, they were powerless to offend, if they had been so inclined. In 1810, a man, named Jorgensen, landed from an English vessel, and set himself up as " Protector of Iceland;" his arbitrary rule was for a time submitted to, but he was soon removed, and sent as a malefactor to Denmark.

In 1848, there was a slight revolutionary outbreak, because Iceland demanded a constitution; the king sent one through the Governor, but the people, assembled at the Althing, disdaining even to read the royal plan, began to frame one for themselves. Finding them determined not to take the king's proposition as a basis, he dissolved the assembly amid great confusion. In the words of Chambers, "A kind of revolution followed, and it became necessary to send an army to restore tranquillity. The army consisted of a lieutenant and thirty-six men; and after its appearance the disturbance ceased."

After the most oppressive commercial regulations in favor of Danish monopolists, in 1854 a system of free trade was introduced, all imposts being abolished, except a trifling tonnage duty. Commerce at once revived; the material resources of the country were developed; the population increased; the value of the exports was quadrupled. While the people thus gained in every way, the Danish merchants have not been losers, though the emoluments of the trade have been divided among a greater number of individuals, most of whom are Danes, who apparently care little for the prosperity of the country which enriches them.

The position of governor of Iceland is not an enviable one, especially if he be surrounded by a rising family. He is expected to serve five years, the salary is not more than that of a first-class clerk with us, and life there is a kind of banishment, in payment for which the incumbent for the full term is regarded as having earned the right to expect a more valuable position from the home government.

The present governor Finssen is an accomplished gentleman, with a charming family, and is popular with all classes. During the royal visit we were indebted to him for many acts of graceful courtesy.

He is liked as well as any Dane can be liked by this people, who think the management of their affairs should be in the hands of native Icelanders, chosen by themselves. A foreign governor, however well disposed, cannot sympathize fully with the desires and needs of the island, and must, of necessity, often find his duty to Denmark in conflict with what justice and expediency claim for Iceland.

DR. HJALTALIN, REYKJAVIK.

CHAPTER XIV.

DISCOVERY OF AMERICA.

"Let us remember Leif Erikson, the first white man who planted his feet on American soil ! Let us remember his brother, Thorwald Erikson, the first European and the first Christian who was buried beneath American sod ! Let us not forget Thorfinn and Gudrid, who established the first European colony in America ! nor their little son, Snorre, the first man of European blood whose birthplace was in the New World ! "

THE above quotation from Professor Anderson's book, entitled " America not discovered by Columbus," published in 1874, indicates a channel of investigation in which several Scandinavian scholars have recently been working with great industry. Though they have proved beyond a doubt that America was known to Europeans centuries before the time of Columbus, they do not, for reasons hereafter stated, in my opinion, diminish in the least the fame

10

of the great Genoese navigator, nor authorize us to deny that he was practically, as far as the progress of nations is concerned, the discoverer of America.

Among the races which reached the American continent before the Norse discovery, may be mentioned the following : according to Strabo, the Greek philosopher, Pytheas, crossed the Atlantic Ocean three hundred and forty years before Christ; but it is most likely that he only went to Thule, one of the northern islands beyond Great Britain. The Phenicians were experienced navigators, and had colonized at a very early period the Canaries ; and they could easily, and doubtless did, reach the American coast.

A recent work claims that this country was discovered in the fifth century by Chinese Buddhist priests ; and it is altogether probable that there was an early communication between America and Asia, and perhaps a distinct settling of the former by way of Behring's Straits. The people of the Aleutian or Fox islands differ from the other inhabitants of the north-west coast in appearance and customs, and are more like those farther south, in Mexico. Many questions of great ethnological interest are here suggested, the discussion of which cannot be attempted here ; such as the origin of the California Indians, of the Aztecs, Central Americans, Inca Peruvians, and Mound Builders, as contrasted with the American Indians to the east, north, and south. It would, indeed, be strange if the modern Icelanders, with their eastern characteristics, coming westward across the Atlantic, should on our Alaskan coast or northwest territories complete the ethnological circle, the western meeting the eastern wave of the nations, which renders American ethnology such a complex study.

There is also good reason to believe that the Irish, or other Pictish race, Roman Catholics, went to America as early as 795, going even as far south as Florida. The Basque fishermen also very early were in the habit of visiting the northern coasts of America in the pursuit of their calling.

What became of these settlers must be left to conjecture; but it is altogether probable that they by degrees became amalgamated with the more numerous surrounding races, — some of them maintaining a splendid existence in Mexico, Central America, and Peru, even to the time of the Spanish conquests; but most of them perishing, leaving no trace except certain customs, words, and traditions among the American Indians, otherwise quite inexplicable.

To Icelanders, among others, belongs the honor of discovering Greenland and America. Günnbjorn, about 880, driven to the west by a storm first sighted Greenland. In 982, Erik the Red sailed there, explored the coast for three years, taking possession of the best places, and spoke of the country, which he called Greenland, on his return, in such terms, that, in 986, quite a colony settled there; they kept up a regular communication with Iceland, only two hundred miles distant, and from land to land very much less. About the year 1000 several Christian churches were established there, with their bishop. Says Professor Anderson : "The discovery of Greenland was a natural consequence of the settlement of Iceland, just as the discovery of America afterwards was a natural consequence of the settlement of Greenland." The colony established after Erik's return was a flourishing one, with Gardar for the capital, and became subject to Norway in 1261; during its continuance no less than seventeen bishops served in Greenland. After a period of more than three hundred and fifty years' intercourse with Norway, Sweden, and Denmark, in 1406 the last bishop was sent over; and from that date nothing was heard from the settlers. Their fate is a mystery as great as that of Sir John Franklin; if they lived on the east coast, as some suppose, the drift ice probably came down upon them, destroying them by cold and starvation; if on the west coast, where the Danish settlements now are, they were more likely exterminated by disease, misery, and the attacks of the Esquimaux. In the beginning of the last century, when the country was again taken possession of by Europeans, the remains of old dwellings were found on the west coast.

America, also, was discovered in 986 by an Icelander, Bjarne Herjulfson, who, the first European, during a voyage to Greenland, was driven out into the Atlantic by a storm; after sailing some days, he came to a wooded land, with alternating hills and plains along the barren coast, probably from Nantucket to Newfoundland; as he could not prevail on his crew to go on shore, he returned to Greenland, with a fair wind, in six days. His and other Norse discoveries of Greenland and America we know from the "Codex Flatæensis," finished in 1387. His description of the country led Leif, son of Erik the Red, to sail from Norway to find it. To the south-west of Greenland he discovered land, believed to have been the coast of Labrador; and farther to the south the wooded country seen by Bjarne, supposed to be Newfoundland, called by him Helluland; farther south what he called Markland, probably Nova Scotia. Two days after, with a strong north-west wind, he came to an island, separated from the mainland by a strait; sailing through this he came to a beautiful inland sea, on whose shores he spent the winter. The sea swarmed with fine salmon, and the grass remained green all winter. On the shortest day the sun was nine hours above the horizon (or from 7.30 A.M. to 4.30 P.M.), which would make the latitude reached a little north of New York ; the island was probably Nantucket, and the inland sea a bay between Rhode Island and Cape Cod. From the discovery of wild grapes there, he called the country Vinland. This was in the year 1000 ; he was the first European known to have stood upon the continent of America ; he passed most of his time in the vicinity, probably, of Mount Hope Bay, R. I., or the present Fall River, in about lat. 41° 24′. His brother, Thorwald, two years after, visited the place, but was killed by the natives (Skrælings or Esquimaux), with whom, however, a settlement, planted soon after by Thorfinn, traded for two hundred years ; the last named evidently went farther south, as he found maize growing wild ; and it is believed that these Northmen went as far as Chesapeake Bay ; and in the traditions of the old Indian tribes of Florida there are indications of white men, possessing iron instruments, having inhabited their country. Thorwald, who lived in America three years, was the first European recorded as having died and been buried here. Thorfinn Karlsefne, who married Gudrid, widow of Thorstein, a younger brother of Thorwald, sailed with her to Vinland, in 1007, from Iceland. He took with him a hundred and fifty-one men and seven women, with a number of cattle and sheep; he remained there three years, when the hostility of the natives compelled them to depart. In 1008 was born to him a son, Snorre Thorfinnson, on the shore of Buzzard's Bay; from this, as far as known, first European born in America was descended the famous Icelander, the sculptor Thorwaldsen, born seven and a half centuries later. Intercourse with these American settlements was kept up till the middle of the fourteenth century, when they seem to have disappeared, either amalgamated with the savage tribes, or destroyed in the wars in which the Esquimaux were forced north by the more warlike tribes which had possession of the country when Columbus first landed.

According to Professor Rafn, who has paid the greatest attention to American antiquities of the Norse occupation, it is set down as a fact that Europeans knew of this country long before Columbus; and he suggests that some of the people living here at the time of his discovery were descendants of Europeans, and that Christianity had been introduced here, both among Norsemen and the Indians, long before this period.

Says also Humboldt, in his "Cosmos," while the Caliphat "of Bagdad was still flourishing under the Abbasides, and while the rule of the Samanides, so favorable to poetry, still flourished in Persia, America was discovered, about the year 1000, by Leif, son of Erik the Red, at about 41½° north latitude."

Professor Anderson, of Madison, Wisconsin, a Scandinavian, has given, in his work before quoted, some of the conclusions of Professor Rafn on the Norse remains in Massachusetts; these he enlarges upon with approval, and it seems to me that the convictions of such experts ought to weigh more with the general scholar and reader than the doubts and objections of iconoclast historians, who have no more respect for Faust and Tell and Thorfinn and Shakspeare than they have for Jack the Giant-killer, St. Nicholas, or the Man in the Moon.

On the famous Dighton rock, in Taunton river, besides undoubted Indian marks, Professor Rafn has discovered the following inscription:

ORFINN, CXXXI, N 〜〜〜 M, NAM,

which he interprets thus: "Thorfinn, with a hundred and fifty-one Norse seafaring men, took possession of this land;" other marks on the rock remove all doubt in his mind. The above Roman numerals represent, according to Professor Anderson, a hundred and fifty-one, the exact number of Thorfinn's party, as the Icelanders reckoned twelve decades to a hundred, calling it "great hundred;" C would, therefore, represent a hundred and twenty instead of a hundred.

The facts, as above interpreted, are stated in the sagas of a character admitted authentic by Scandinavian scholars, and no others have any right to decide the matter. From the same sources we are told that the Icelanders made other expeditions, as far south as Florida, and up to near the end of the fourteenth century, when they were arrested by the ravages of the fearful " black plague," which devastated northern Europe and Iceland.

In 1831, a skeleton in brass armor was disinterred near Fall River, Massachusetts, which attracted much attention at the time, and caused much learned discussion ; it suggested to Professor Longfellow, in 1841, the poem beginning : —

"Speak ! speak ! thou fearful guest ! "

The chemist Berzelius analyzed a portion of the breastplate, and found it to consist of 98⅓ per cent of copper (70.29) and zinc (28.03), with 0.91 tin, 0.74 lead, and 0.03 iron, — coming much nearer the composition of the old Denmark bronzes of the tenth century than to the alloys of the eighteenth ; the breastplate also agreed with this portion of the old northern armors. Says Professor Anderson : " The circumstances connected with it are so wonderful that it might indeed seem almost as though it were the skeleton of this very Thorwald Erikson ! " and yet

10*   o

there are those so incredulous as to intimate that these are the remains of an American Indian, buried with pieces of a comparatively modern brass kettle!

Some believe that we find traces of the Norse settlements in the "old tower" at Newport, Rhode Island, whose origin and purpose have long been a mystery; it resembles other structures left by them in the Orkney and Shetland Islands. It is thus alluded to in the poem of Longfellow above quoted : —

> " Three weeks we westward bore,
> And when the storm was o'er,
> Cloudlike we saw the shore
> Stretching to leeward ;
> There for my lady's bower
> Built I the lofty tower,
> Which to this very hour
> Stands looking seaward."

Professor Anderson says that the Newport tower " undoubtedly was built by the Norsemen," and that " the Indians told the early New England settlers [it] was built by the giants, and the Norse discoverers certainly looked like giants to the Indians." On the other hand, it is maintained that the tower was built by governor Arnold, of Rhode Island, for a windmill, to replace one of wood blown down in a storm ; various specious reasons are given for the peculiarity of the construction, which, to my mind, are quite as difficult to accept as the explanation of the antiquarians. Whether built by Norsemen or Englishmen, it is strange that the early annals of the colony do not make frequent mention of so strange a structure, and that, if built in such modern time as governor Arnold's, there should be any possible question in the matter. Governor Arnold very likely built a stone windmill, but that it now stands as the "Newport Tower" is by no means certainly established; there is much mystery and doubt in the matter, and I prefer, with the Scandinavian antiquarians and scholars, to give the benefit of the doubt to the Norsemen, who so long inhabited this very region in America.

Now that the historical relations of Iceland to America have been given, the reader is referred back to the poetic greeting of Bayard Taylor, on page 78, the appropriateness of whose personages and events will now be more fully appreciated.

There is also evidence from the Sagas, that the Welsh, under Madoc, colonized America in 1170; this adds another perplexing element to the problem of American archæology.

It is, therefore, beyond a doubt that America was known to Europeans five hundred years before Columbus set foot upon its islands. From his own letter, as quoted by Washington Irving, it appears that this celebrated navigator was in Iceland in 1477, only one hundred and thirty years after the last Norse expedition thither ; and Humboldt, in his Cosmos, regards it as a fact that he got at Reykjavik in that year the information from the Icelandic manuscripts which led him to cross the Atlantic. Whether he did or did not learn any thing in Iceland about America is, of course, uncertain ; but he *could* have consulted there the accounts of Leif's voyage, written at least one hundred years before his first voyage ; and it is fair to presume that such a shrewd observer *would not* have neglected such an excellent opportunity.

Other facts, collected by Professor Anderson, showing that Columbus probably knew of the "land to the west of Europe," are, 1. The opportunity to consult maps in Rome: Gudrid, wife of Thorfinn, after the death of her husband, made a pilgrimage to Rome, and personally communicated a knowledge of Vinland ; pope Paschal II., in 1112, appointed Erik Upsi bishop of Iceland, Greenland, and Vinland, and he went to the last in 1121. 2. Adam of Bremen's writings, published in 1073, make mention of Vinland ; and Columbus, like other students of geography, in an age of maritime discovery by England, France, Spain, and Portugal, must have known of and examined them. His conviction of the existence of land beyond the Atlantic, was founded, on his own avowal, on the authority of "learned writers," and did not arise at all either from accident or inspiration.

It seems to me that Columbus never entertained an idea of discovering a *new world*, as he must have known that the rediscovery of a continent, visited by the Northmen for five hundred years, would avail him nothing ; he was in search of a very different thing ; viz., a western route to India, — a commercial and not a geographical problem he wished to solve. He thought that Cuba and Haiti, which he discovered on his first voyage, were parts of the eastern extremity of Asia ; hence he called these the Indies, and their people Indians ; to which the term West was added, to distinguish them from the East Indies. He touched at Jamaica on his second voyage, which he found inhabited by fierce cannibal Caribs, so different from the other American Indians, that it has been thought that they came across the Atlantic and not the Pacific.

Far be it from me, in the above statements, to detract in the least from the genius and merit of Columbus ; though America had been discovered a thousand years before his day, such knowledge and occupation were of no practical use to the world ; and not until his voyages, whatever their object might have been, were the movements of human races directed for permanent benefit to man to the New World. Therefore, all honor to Columbus for his discovery of America, which had better have been called Columbia.

Many a man had seen the lid of a tea-kettle raised by the enclosed vapor, but James Watt first utilized the power of steam in a practical way ; many a college professor and physician knew that the vapor of sulphuric ether would produce insensibility and deep sleep, but no one demonstrated the fact that it could be safely used for the annihilation of pain in severe surgical operations until Dr. W. T. G. Morton's experiments in the Massachusetts General Hospital in 1846 ; many scientific men were acquainted with the possibility of sending signals along electric wires for short distances, but Morse is none the less the inventor of the electric telegraph.

Not to the one who first discovers a thing, and allows it to lie idle in his brain, but to him who first renders it of use to the world, will the honor of the discovery justly be attributed. The laurels, then, need not be taken from the brow of Columbus, and placed upon the head of the Icelander Leif, the son of Erik. Both should be crowned.

The Norse colonies all died out, but the possession of fire-arms enabled the Spaniards to maintain their ground against the hosts of the naked and poorly armed Indians. Says Professor Anderson : " If the communication between Vinland and the north could have been maintained say one hundred years longer, that is, to the middle of the fifteenth century, it is difficult to determine what the result would have been. Possibly this sketch would have appeared in *Icelandic* instead of English. Undoubtedly the Norse colonies would have become firmly rooted by that time, and Norse language, nationality, and institutions might have played as conspicuous a part in America as the English and their posterity do now-a-days."

CHAPTER XV.

LITERATURE OF ICELAND.

LITERARY AND HEROIC AGE. — EDDAS AND SAGAS. — THE SKALDS. —
HEIMSKRINGLA. — LANDNAMABOK. — ICELANDIC POETRY. — VALUE
OF ICELANDIC LITERATURE IN THE ESTIMATION OF SCHOLARS.
— LANGUAGE, AND ITS RELATIONS TO THE ANGLO-SAXON. —
LORD'S PRAYER IN NORSE. — EDUCATION OF THE PEOPLE. —
JOHN THORLAKSON. — SCHOOLS. — NEWSPAPERS. — LIBRARY AT
REYKJAVÍK. — THORWALDSEN'S FONT.

" Thou recallest bards,
  Who, in solitary chambers,
  And with hearts by passion wasted,
  Wrote thy pages.

Thou recallest homes,
  Where thy songs of love and friendship
  Made the gloomy northern winter
  Bright as summer.

Once some ancient skald,
  In his bleak ancestral Iceland,
  Chanted staves of these old ballads
  To the Vikings."

IT is singular that, while the rest of Europe was
immersed in intellectual darkness, this cold and
barren island should have been the workshop and the
repository in which the most important events of the
age, in all parts of northern Europe, were rescued from

oblivion. The history of their Norwegian ancestors, and of their own warlike deeds, was preserved and recited in the verses of the native skalds or poets, attached to the persons of the high chiefs ; and thus events, crowded out of memory by the bloody wars of the continent, were preserved in this more peaceful island, which thus became the historic storehouse of the past and the present. These poems, or sagas, as they were called, were recited both in public meetings and in family gatherings of the high and low, and thus became the property of the whole people. The older sagas were mythical, but the later ones historical, and authentic, even minute, records of actual events. The language is generally pure and elegant, as among the Scandinavian nations the eloquent tongue commanded equal honor with the valiant hand.

Poetry seems always to have preceded prose ; as rhythm, rhyme, and measured lines are more easily remembered and recited, and listened to with more pleasure for their bold imagery, than irregular or monotonous prose. The measure of the Icelandic poetic works is often very complicated ; their chief characteristic ornament was alliteration, which seems almost peculiar to the northern nations ; their rhymes often occurred in the middle of the lines, and even in the middle of words, and in many respects resembled the Anglo-Saxon, another branch of the Teutonic stock.

They were not only committed to memory, but were engraved on wood in Runic characters, and in Roman letters after the introduction of Christianity. These skalds were noble and warlike men, who, like the troubadours, wandered into foreign lands, everywhere received with honor, and in this way brought back the knowledge of the most important occurrences in Europe, from Russia to the Mediterranean, the East, and the Holy Land, which, after the custom of the country, were preserved in the written sagas.

In the " Heimskringla," or " Orb of the World," of Snorre Sturleson, and the Edda by the same author, we find a continuous and consistent history of his own and the continental nations in the simple Icelandic language. It has been said that " to this work we are indebted for our chief knowledge of those Norman chiefs, whose names made the kings of Europe tremble in their palaces, and whose descendants now sit on the mightiest of their thrones." Of this, Longfellow speaks in his Saga of King Olaf, as follows : —

> " A wondrous book
> Of legends in the old Norse tongue, —
> Legends that once were told or sung
> In many a smoky fireside nook
> Of Iceland, in the ancient day,
> By wandering saga-man or skald ;
> Heimskringla is the volume called."

Translations of the first are found in Danish and Latin, and of the second in Mallett's "Northern Antiquities." Older than these were the writings of Are Frode and Sæmund Frode, of which Snorre has made great use. After Snorre came Sturle Thordsson, his brother-in-law, who, in 1284, wrote the history of the island during the twelfth and thirteenth centuries, until its subjection to the Norwegian kings.

The most curious of all is the "Landnamabok," the narrative of the origin and progress of the Icelandic nation, written by various authors, from Are Frode, in the latter part of the eleventh century, to Erlendsen, in the beginning of the fourteenth. It contains the names of about three thousand persons and fourteen hundred places, and is the most complete genealogical record of a nation in existence. This, with the historical sagas, has been published by the Society of Northern Antiquaries of Copenhagen, in Danish and Latin. Several modern poets have selected these sagas as the subjects for their poems, and among them Longfellow, whose name is dearly loved, as I had frequent opportunity to know, by these warm-hearted Icelanders.

It will be seen from these statements that the principal and most interesting monuments of Iceland are her literary ones. These present to the modern scholar the most complete account of Scandinavian mythology in the older poetic and younger prose Eddas, — the former being a collection of the fragments of the ancient myths current in the twelfth century; the latter, or younger, being a historical compilation, amplifying and supplementing the former. The name of sagas is generally understood as belonging to the legendary accounts of events which occurred in Norway and Iceland from the ninth to the thirteenth century, mixed with much metaphorical and intricate versification, exceedingly puzzling to scholars.

According to Baring Gould, who has made the sagas a special study, Icelandic poetry has gone through four stages : 1. The Edda period, with a simple metre, and plain and vigorous language ; 2. That of the "verse-smiths," who hammered out stanzas full of epithet and simile, but very obscure in meaning ; 3. That of ballads, mostly reproductions of well-known popular songs of various nations ; 4. Of the "rimur," the sagas set to jingling rhyme coming into vogue during the last century, and still popular, generally chanted to slow and solemn melody.

Almost every traveller who has been to Iceland, and has published any account thereof, gives examples of these sagas ; any interested in these myths are referred to Baring Gould's "Iceland : its Scenes and Sagas." London : 1863 ; and to Professor An-

derson's recently published " Norse Mythology."
Many of the popular superstitions and nursery tales
of the past and present English-speaking races are
of Icelandic origin. " Mother Goose " is largely
Scandinavian; "Jack and Gill," "Dickery, dickery,
dock," and many others, were well known to the
Norsemen.

Most of the recent Icelandic literature is of a serious and even devotional character ; and their poetic
translations are mainly selected from such authors as
Homer, Shakespeare, Milton, Klopstock, and Pope.

There can be no doubt that Icelandic literature is
a mine of wealth, which has been sadly neglected by
scholars, and cultivated only by a select few. Professor Anderson, at the end of his book on the discovery of America, gives copious extracts from American,
English, and German authors, expressing their high
opinion of the historical, linguistic, and literary value
of the Scandinavian languages, now spoken in purity
only in Iceland. He says himself : " I will add that I
have not found a scholar, who has devoted himself to
this field of study and research, that has not at the
same time become an enthusiastic admirer of Scandinavian, and particularly Icelandic history, languages,
and literatures."

The following is from Professor W. Fiske, the most
learned cultivator of these northern languages in this

country : " It [the old Icelandic literature] deserves
the careful study of every student of letters.   For the
English-speaking races, especially, there is nowhere,
so near home, a field promising to the scholar so rich
a harvest.   The few translations, or attempted translations, which are to be found in English, give
merely a faint idea of the treasures of antique wisdom and sublime poetry which exist in the Eddic
lays, or of the quaint simplicity, dramatic action,
and striking realism which characterize the historical
sagas."

From B. F. De Costa, he quotes : " Yet while other
nations were without a literature, the intellect of Iceland was in active exercise, and works were produced
like the Eddas and Heimskringla, works which, being
inspired by a lofty genius, will rank with the writings
of Homer and Herodotus."

The Howitts say : " There is nothing, besides the
Bible and the poem of Homer itself, which can com-
pare in all the elements of greatness with the Edda.
The Icelandic poems have no parallel in all the treasures of ancient literature ; they are the expressions
of the souls of poets existing in the primeval and un-
effeminated earth.   The Edda is a structure of that
grandeur and importance, that it deserves to be far
better known to us generally than it is.   The spirit
in it is sublime and colossal."

Professor Longfellow says : " The Icelandic is as remarkable as the Anglo-Saxon for its abruptness, its obscurity, and the boldness of its metaphors. Poets are called Songsmiths ; poetry, the Language of the Gods; gold, the Daylight of Dwarfs ; the rainbow, the Bridge of the Gods ; a battle, a Bath of Blood, the Hail of Odin, the Meeting of Shields ; the tongue, the Sword of Words ; rivers, the Sweat of Earth, the Blood of the Valleys; arrows, the Daughters of Misfortune, the Hailstones of Helmets ; the earth, the Vessel that floats on the Ages ; the sea, the Field of Pirates ; a ship, the Skate of Pirates, the Horse of the Waves. When the long winter came, the poet bewailed the death of Baldr, the sun ; and he saw in each eclipse the horrid form of the wolf, Managamr, who swallowed the moon and stained the sky with blood."

Professor Anderson's " Norse Mythology " (1875) is the first complete and systematic presentation of the subject in the English language, and will be heartily welcomed as filling an important gap in English literature, and as a delightful companion for the student in his walks amid the mysterious and weird halls of Scandinavian antiquity.

In the dialect of the people of the Orkneys are many words of Scandinavian origin; the old Norse has also entered largely into the formation of the

Lowland Scotch; as the Scandinavian and Anglo-Saxon languages are branches of the old Gothic stem, many words in Norse and modern English are essentially the same; in the parts of Great Britain settled by Celts, as Scotland, most of the local names betray a Celtic origin, while Norse names prevail in the regions invaded by Norwegians and Danes.

The following are a few Icelandic words, selected from a long list given by Mackenzie, in 1810, to show their resemblance to English: *eyrn*, one; *tveir*, two; *thryr*, three; *fioorer*, four; *sex*, six; *aatta*, eight; *twolf*, twelve; *threttan*, thirteen; *fioortan*, fourteen; *hundrad*, hundred; *thusund*, thousand. Common words in both languages are: back, bane, bed, spade; *barn*, child; *blad*, blade; *blek*, black; *fader*, father; *faede*, food; *fie*, money; *fingur*, finger; *foolk*, folks; *hæna*, hen; *hagl*, hail; *hlaatur*, laughter; *hlaup*, leap; *molld*, mould; *ol*, ale; *thif*, thief; *torf*, turf; and *tuinne*, twine.

These examples could be multiplied indefinitely, but these few are enough to show how intimately connected are the Norse and English languages, and how necessary to the English philologist is the study of the Scandinavian tongue.

In the preface to Mallet's "Northern Antiquities," may be found the Lord's Prayer in a Norse dialect, which is still intelligible even in the Orkney islands: —

Favor ihr i Chimrie. Helleut   ir Nam thite. Gi:la cosdum
Father our in Heaven. Hallowed be name thine. Kingdom

thite cumma. Veya thine mota var gort o Yurn sinna gort
thine come.   Will thine may be done on earth as   done

i Chimrie. Gav vus Da on Da dalight Brow vora. Foigive
in Heaven. Give us day and day daily bread our.   Forgive

vus Sinna   vora s n vee foigive Sindara mutha vus. Lyv
us offences our as we forgive offences amongst us.   Lead

vus ye i Tumtation. Min delivera vus fro olt Ilt. Amen.
us not in temptation. But deliver us from all ill. Amen.

The present mental cultivation of the people is very high. Education is carried on at home by parents during the long winter evenings, under the supervision of the clergymen. The common people are well acquainted with their own and other national histories, ancient and modern ; they know all about the early discovery of America by the Northmen, five centuries before Columbus, while very few of us, until recently, knew any more of Iceland than we did of the South Pole or the wilds of Africa.

To show the extent of the education of the people, and the unassuming character of Icelandic scholars, I will mention two incidents that occurred during our trip, one of which is alluded to in Bayard Taylor's recently published description of it.

One of our guides, Geir by name, a poor, fatherless

boy of seventeen, we knew spoke English very well,
and when at a loss for a word or its meaning would
inquire what it was in Latin. He then surprised Mr.
Taylor by the question, " What do you think of Byron
as a poet ? Is not the song of the spirits, in " Manfred,"
considered very fine ? " This lad spoke German about
as fluently as he did English ; he had read the ballads
of Schiller, and his " Robbers," and wanted to know
if Faust, which he had heard was difficult to understand, was any thing like in style to Shakspeare, whose
" King Lear " he had read. What lad of seventeen
among us, with all our boasted advantages, could
stand by the side of this boy, who had never been off
Iceland !

A party of Englishmen who followed us had engaged with some difficulty guides to the Geysers, —
one of them a modest, sedate, worthy man, whose
movements were not of so rapid a character, nor his
attentions so constant as they thought they ought to
be ; they scolded at him, which made him more reserved and inattentive, and finally they became so
angry that they swore at him. He understood English perfectly well, and the moment he heard the
oaths, he was so indignant that he turned round and
left them to find their way with their other guide.
On asking him why the man behaved so strangely,
he said that he was not in the habit of being spoken

to in such an uncivil manner. He was one of the first historians of Iceland, and had offered his services to the strangers as a friend and not as a servant.

The study of the classics is very general, and the traveller is, as we were, often surprised to find persons in humble life able to converse in Latin. As a type of an Icelandic scholar may be mentioned John Thorlakson, who, beside being the author of many original poems, translated Milton's "Paradise Lost" into Eddaic verse ; he was poor and obliged to labor for a living ; though a clergyman for two parishes his whole income therefrom was only forty dollars a year, and from this he had to pay an assistant. In his small, dark room, with little hope that it would ever be published, this poor scholar executed his work, which, for purity and beauty of language, and grandeur of imagery (for it is rather a paraphrase than a translation), would put to shame many publications done up in morocco, gilt, and tinted paper. He also translated Pope's "Essay on Man," and Klopstock's "Messiah." He died in 1819. I have also "Macbeth" translated into Icelandic by a native scholar (Matthias Jochumsson), published in 1874.

It has been stated that, owing to the scattered population, public schools are out of the question in Iceland, the ordinary education of the people being

secured by teaching at home during the long winters, seconded by the taste for reading which is universal. There is, however, a school at Reykjavik for
the advanced education of a selected number of native
youth ; there is accommodation for about sixty, and
the pupils are carried as far as in our high schools ;
the class-rooms are well equipped, and special attention is paid to the modern languages, Latin, and
mathematics. Being a government institution, no
fees are charged, and only promising students are
permitted to enjoy its advantages ; those wishing to
prepare themselves for the learned professions of the
law, medicine, and theology pass on to enter the university at Copenhagen.

There are in the capital several modern printing-
presses, which do excellent work, both in the way of
books and newspapers ; of course, in a country almost
impassable for half the year, news cannot travel very
fast, and the newspaper is not the record of the present, every-day world that it is with us ; hence, ac-
curate information in regard to the recent terrible
devastation by the volcanic eruption in the Vatna
Jokul region was very slow in coming even to the
capital, and still slower in getting across the ice-
bound ocean to Europe ; several months of great
suffering were passed before any helping hand could
be raised from abroad for the unfortunates.

One of the most interesting features of their apparatus for popular education is the library in the upper story of the church at Reykjavik. It contains a few thousand volumes, most of them presents, in all languages, especially Danish, Icelandic, and English; there are no old manuscripts of any great value, and few costly books, the library being for popular use, on payment of less than a dollar a year; the books are widely circulated, and the privilege is much prized by the people. There are many standard English and American works, especially in history, poetry, and fiction, with several publications of the American government. Complaints were loud at the capital that large numbers of books sent by governments, business houses, and private individuals, are stopped in Copenhagen, and never reach their destination in Iceland. There were very large contributions sent at the time of the millennial celebration, through the agency of the Smithsonian Institution, it was said: such as went by way of England most likely arrived; such as passed into Denmark probably were somewhat curtailed.

Iceland has nothing to boast of in the way of art, unless she may claim the sculptor Thorwaldsen, born at sea of an Icelandic father, his grandfather having been the parish priest at Miklibaer. The baptismal font presented by him to the church at Reykjavik, and to be seen there now, is in the form of a low square obelisk, having in front a representation of the baptism of Jesus; on the left, one of the Virgin and Child, with the infant John on her knee; on the right, Jesus blessing little children; on the back is a group of angels surmounting the inscription : *Opus hoc Romæ fecit, et Islandiæ, terræ sibi gentiliaceæ, pietatis causâ, donavit Albertus Thorvaldsen, anno* MDCCCXXVII.

CHAPTER XVI.

VOLCANIC HISTORY OF ICELAND.

EXTENT OF JOKULS. — TRAP. — OSCILLATIONS OF THE SOIL. —
ELLBORG. — ERUPTIVE PERIODS. — LINE OF VOLCANIC ENERGY.
— NUMBER OF GREAT ERUPTIONS. — GLACIERS. — KRABLA. —
KATLUGIA, AND ITS FLOODS OF WATER. — SKAPTAR JOKUL. —
HECLA, AND ITS ERUPTIONS. — ASCENT OF HECLA. — VATNA
JOKUL, AND THE TERRIBLE ERUPTION OF 1874-75. — DESTITU-
TION OF THE PEOPLE. — FORMS OF LAVA. — CAUSES OF VOL-
CANOES. — THEORIES OF CENTRAL FIRE, CHEMICAL ACTION,
AND ACCUMULATIONS WITHIN THE CRUST OF THE EARTH. —
MALLET'S THEORY OF SHRINKING OF THE CRUST, AND CON-
VERSION OF THIS MOTION INTO HEAT.

> " Hearken, thou craggy jokul pyramid !
> When were thy shoulders hid in icy streams ?
> How long is 't since the mighty power bid
> Thee heave to airy sleep from fathom dreams ?
> Thou answer'st not, for thou art dead asleep ;
> Thy life is but two dead eternities, —
> The last in air, the former in the deep ;
> Drowned wast thou till an earthquake made thee steep ;
> Volcanic Vatna, with thy giant size ! "

THE tract we passed over on our road to Thingvalla, was the work of the volcano of the Skald
Breid, or Broad Shield ; but the whole island has, in one
part or another, been torn by volcanic agency, and all
the mountains seem to be in a state of intermittent
activity liable to break out at any time. The volcanic

history of the island, therefore, is exceedingly interesting, but space will not permit me to enlarge upon it.

Small as the cultivable land of Iceland must have
been since its occupation, fire, water, and ice from its
jokuls have considerably lessened it ; they are found
everywhere, but especially in the south-east, where
a mass of ice, with a few interruptions, rests on a
cluster of dormant volcanic cones, occupying a space
of at least three thousand square miles, and from
three to six thousand feet high, among them the
famous Breidamark, Oræfa, and Skaptar.

The oldest of the rocks is a basalt, or trap, horizontal, upheaved beneath the sea, probably toward the
end of the tertiary epoch ; over this a tufaceous, less
solid and spongy trachyte, which has been thrust up
through the trap, and highest, the comparatively
modern lavas, formed in the air, the oldest believed to
date from the glacial period.   Iceland and Jan Meyen
have been the volcanic centres in the basin of the
northern ocean, Norway on the east and Greenland
on the west showing the primitive rocks of gneiss,
granite, and mica slates.   In the trachyte formation
are situated the jokuls and volcanoes, in a line running
from south-west to north-east, with numerous interruptions and outlying spurs.   The trap formation
covers more than half the island, and with an average
thickness of two thousand five hundred feet, showing

what an immense mass of fluid matter has here issued from the earth.

There have, probably, been several periods of volcanic activity, though geologists differ as to the number, duration, and precise epoch, during which the basalts of Iceland and the overlying trachyte, or palagonite have been upheaved. Indeed, some of the characters of Iceland scenery are noticed by the traveller, whether he sail from eastern Scotland, as we did, or from Norway ; the hills from Edinburgh, northward, bear evidence in their forms and structure of volcanic action, though at a period doubtless anterior to the uplifting of Iceland above the sea.

There must, also, have been several oscillations of the soil. Near Husavik, in the north, high up in a tufaceous deposit, is a huge mineralized whale skeleton, whose ribs are exposed ; and at a height of two hundred feet above the present sea level are beds of the shell, *Venus Islandica*, in immense numbers. A hundred yards inland is found buried a dark-colored drift-wood, tough, but not yet converted into lignite, of at least ten different kinds from the American shores. The occurrence of such timber on the coasts of Iceland and the Faroes was known in the time of Columbus ; and one would think that his sagacity would from that alone have penetrated the secret of the existence of "land to the west." Within the memory

11*

of persons now living, the coast on the north and west has risen so as to change navigable waters ànd fiords into shallow bays.

The first eruption of which there is a historic record, is that of the Ellborg, or Fortress of Fire, in the western part of the island, which was active in the ninth or tenth century ; it is about one hundred miles north of the capital and fifteen miles from the coast. It stands amid its lava ruins, which display every shade of color, variety of form, and degree of roughness, — a vitrified sea, looking as if thousands of gigantic " glass-blowers had chosen this as the scene of their labors ; " it is a cinder and ash hill, about six hundred feet in diameter, crowned with a fortress of dark lava, like a giant's tower, and two hundred feet high.

In the year 1000 occurred the eruption to the south-west of Thingvalla, whose accompanying earthquakes were felt and heard during the debate before alluded to, which resulted in the displacement of heathenism by catholicism. From this to the end of the fourteenth century, Hecla, and others to the north and south, were active, with destructive earthquakes. They were quiet for more than one hundred years, when, after a short activity, occurred another period of repose till the eighteenth century, in which Krabla in the north, and Hecla, Katlugia, and Skaptar in the south, were in violent operation. From 1783 to 1821, there was quiet, when Eyafialla in the south was active for six months, bursting its icy covering, and deluging the surrounding country with water, mud, lava, and ashes ; Katlugia became again eruptive, covering a thousand square miles.

According to the observations of the experienced Dr. Hjaltalin, of Reykjavik, eruptions in Iceland are almost always preceded by fine weather. The preceding earthquake shocks always travel in a northeast to south-west direction, or *vice versâ;* seeming to indicate that this is the line of volcanic energy, to whatever cause due, extending from Jan Meyen on the north to the Azores on the south ; this line passes through the Faroes, the western islands of Scotland; and Great Britain, extending southerly to the Canaries, Cape de Verd islands, Ascension, and St. Helena to Tristan d'Acunha in the latitude of the Cape of Good Hope, a distance of one hundred and twenty degrees of latitude on very nearly the same meridian.

No portion of the world, except the Sandwich and other Pacific islands, has been so often and so terribly convulsed by volcanoes as Iceland. Hecla has erupted thirteen times since the year 1000, and Katlugia fifteen times since 900 ; and the single or few eruptions from other volcanoes have been of unparalleled severity, especially those from the Skaptar and Vatna

jokuls, from the region of the last of which burst out
the eruption of 1874–75, which has desolated some
of the finest portions of the island, as is hereafter
stated.

In the words of a recent traveller : " The volcanoes
of Iceland belong to the class known as paroxysmal,
the most dangerous and treacherous of the whole
family ; since, by long periods of tranquillity, continued sometimes through ages, they lure the surrounding inhabitants into a false idea of security, and
the character of their terrible neighbor is at length
only proclaimed by the sudden outburst, destructive
alike to life and property."

The mountains of Iceland are not high, and their
shapes are well adapted for the collecting the snow
which by its covering constitutes them "jokuls ; " the
action of the sun, and the daily and monthly changes
of temperature, soon convert the snow into ice. The
heavy accumulation above forces the lower portion
of the glacier thus formed through the gorges to the
plains, the irresistible ice-plough tearing up the pasture-lands at their base, an icy torrent in summer
pouring from the end. Should the jokul be a slumbering volcano, as many are, and the fiery energy
become active, floods of hot water, bearing ice, stones,
and mud, overflow the surrounding country, sweeping
man and his property to destruction. One of these

ice fields, the Breidamark, is twenty miles long, fifteen wide, and four hundred feet high, occupying what was prior to the fourteenth century a fertile, thickly inhabited plain. The masses of *débris* thus scattered over the country have done incalculable mischief, desolating whole regions. The influence of these icy masses on the climate of the island has been alluded to, and in an uncommonly cold and wet season their increase is a national disaster, destroying the short summer, and with it all food for domestic animals. These eruptions are not confined to the land, but extend far into the ocean; the Westmann islands, in the range of the southern chain of jokuls, are almost all lava; as are Cape Kejkianess and the adjacent islands, the continuation of the northern chain. There have been great and sudden changes near the coast, and in 1783 an island rose from the sea, disappearing during a violent earthquake in the following year.

Krabla in the north, like Hecla in the south, has made its own crater by successive eruptions; it is surrounded on the plains by pits of boiling, sulphurous mud, evidently in old craters, one described by Henderson being three hundred feet in circumference, — horrible to look at, and dangerous to approach from the fetid gases, soft earth, and numerous pitfalls; it was believed by the natives to communicate with the infernal regions, and was named accordingly.

This was concerned in one of the most violent and prolonged eruptions that has desolated the country, raging for five years, from 1724 to 1730. After a period of quiet for centuries, its old lava being overgrown with moss, it suddenly burst out, its floods dividing into many arms, going along the valleys in various directions, the largest stream being fourteen miles long and two wide, entering a large lake, killing all the fish, and making it boil for many days ; burning up houses and grass lands, but turned aside by trifling obstacles ; attended by sulphurous gases, and glowing at night with lurid flames ; forming galleries and caverns hung with stalactites, from the upper crust hardening, and the fluid parts flowing out underneath ; the appearances, and singularly enough the name, stein-*aa*, being the same as in the eruptions of the Sandwich Islands.

Katlugia, with its present icy covering, looks calmly down on its ruin of centuries of intermittent activity ; it not only destroyed man and beast, but covered up their dwelling-places by successive deluges of water, bearing ice and ashes ; throwing out its lava streams into the sea, and producing islands, since broken up by submarine convulsions into dangerous rocks and shoals.

Again in 1755, a year celebrated for volcanic and earthquake disturbance all the world over, — the year in which Lisbon was destroyed — this volcano burst forth with its floods of hot water, bearing masses of ice and rock, overwhelming more than fifty farms spared by the previous eruption ; the air was filled with stifling smoke, and the thick clouds of ashes enveloped the country in darkness, leaving the soil covered with a waste of sand, gravel, and lava blocks, more destructive, because more widely spread, than the streams of fiery lava. The plains have to some presented the appearances left by the drift of the glacial period, boulders and all, but they have been produced by the above agency of water, and not by ice.

The true glacier, however, we have seen, exists in Iceland, descending from the jokuls into the plains, polishing the underlying rocks, with a moraine at their extremity.

The eruption of Katlugia, in 1869, was described by an eyewitness in the Islendingur newspaper, published in Reykjavik. It began on May 8th, in the morning by earthquakes, which occurred at intervals during the day, followed by a rush of water from the volcano in the afternoon. On the 9th, smoke was seen on the mountain, accompanied by a fall of ashes ; on the 10th, its pumice reached the sea-shore ; on the 11th, the streams of water increased, and fire was visible at night, the showers of ashes continuing and, for the next three days, frost occurring every night. So much sand was poured into the sea, that it formed banks in fifteen fathoms of water; immense pieces of ice were brought down by the flood and stranded in the sea. The snow was all melted off, and the mountain for some time looked black. The eruption lasted three weeks, doing no great harm, except covering considerable meadow land with sand.

The characteristics of the eruptions of Katlugia are the little or no lava, and the immense floods of water thrown out. It is maintained that this water does not come from the inside of the crater, as in the case of the geyser, as flame and water could not coexist in the same cavity; but that it is due to the sudden melting, by subterranean heat, of the vast masses of ice and snow covering the volcanoes of Iceland, as of other snowy regions, in this particular instance, an accumulation of nearly one hundred years.

This explanation is not in all cases entirely satisfactory, inasmuch as other volcanoes, having no covering of snow, have poured out floods of water; in 1631, several villages, with Torre del Greco, were destroyed by a torrent of boiling water accompanying the lava of Vesuvius; in Sicily, in 1790, several fissures sent forth water, with sulphur and other volcanic products; in various parts of the world, and even in Iceland, water has been known to issue from volcanoes uncovered by snow or ice. But in all these cases, there must be some reservoir in which the water is stored, whether from melting snows or surface streams, and let loose, more or less heated, at the time of the eruption. In such cases as Katlugia, the immense floods suddenly poured forth, could hardly be accounted for by the melting of its icy covering, and the reservoir theory would seem entitled to consideration as an accessory explanation.

This volcano has had nine of these hot-water eruptions since its occupation by the Northmen, the destructive one of 1775 occurring after a delusive quiet of thirty-five years, and completely overflowing Myrdalsand ; fifty farms, soil, houses, churches, cattle, horses, and men were actually swept out to sea ; those whose lives were saved were not only deprived of all their possessions, but the very soil was carried away, as if the demon of destruction was determined to drive them from the face of the earth.

The most destructive of all the eruptions on record was that from the Skaptar jokul, eighty miles east of Hecla, about the middle of June, 1783, preceded by violent earthquakes all along the southern coast. It burst out with great fury, drying up the river in twenty-four hours, and filling its bed ; the lava in some places six hundred feet deep and two hundred wide, flowing like a mighty river toward the sea,

wrapping whole districts in flames, remelting old
lavas, opening subterranean caverns, one of its
streams reaching the ocean; it was in full activity for
two months and a half, and did not cease entirely for
six months more. It took the lava more than two
years to cool; one stream was fifty miles long, twelve
to fifteen broad on the plain, and from one to six
hundred feet deep; another was forty miles long and
seven wide; pasture lands one hundred miles around
were destroyed by the pumice, sand, and ashes;
the matter ejected has been estimated at twice the
volume of Mount Hecla, or one hundred thousand
millions of cubic yards, probably as large as any single
mass of the older igneous rocks known to exist;
according to Bischoff, greater than the bulk of Mont
Blanc. Man, his cattle, houses, churches, and grass
lands were burned up; noxious vapors filled the air,
and the earth was shrouded by clouds of ashes;
cattle deprived of grass, and man of fish, perished in
great numbers. At a moderate calculation, more
than twelve hundred human beings, twenty thousand
horses, seven thousand cattle, and one hundred and
thirty thousand sheep perished in this single eruption.

The Oræfa jokul, near the south-east coast, not far
from the place where Ingolf landed in Iceland, in the
latter part of the ninth century, the highest peak in

the island, was the scene of a frightful eruption in 1727.

Mount Hecla presents a great variety of forms, according to the point of view of the observer, but always deserves its name of "cloaked," having usually a mantle of snow, and very often of clouds also. The plain from which it rises is a very fertile one, and contains more farms than any other region of equal size. Its barren and sandy portions, the work of the volcano, are strewn with rounded pebbles, worn by the rapidly shifting waters, the great rainfall, and the attrition of the wind-blown sand.

The view of Mount Hecla from our geyser camp was exceedingly fine, and some of our party would willingly have tried to make the ascent, which, though difficult, cannot be called dangerous. There are several accounts of this feat, one by Madame Pfeiffer, in 1845, and by several persons since. But the inexorable demands of newspaper correspondents, added to the obstacles, real and imaginary, stated to be in the way, such as tortuous and difficult paths, swollen rivers, depth of snow, treacherous bogs, and the evident indisposition of the guides, perhaps from superstitious fears, to make the attempt, compelled us to turn our backs upon this snowy monarch of Iceland.

Hecla is neither the highest nor the most remarkable of these volcanoes ; but it has attracted the most attention, both from natives and strangers, from its situation near the most frequented part of the island, its frequent and disastrous eruptions, and its comparative ease of access. Though only about five thousand feet high, with a circumference of twenty-five miles, it is one of the three great volcanoes of Europe, the others being Vesuvius and Etna. It is isolated, about thirty-five miles inland, and, in clear weather, can be seen from the ocean. It is made up of tufaceous slag, ashes, and pumice, cemented by its own lava streams, and underlaid by a ridge of palagonite, itself the result of submarine volcanic action. It is a member of a ridge of vast extent, belonging to the class of volcanoes arranged in linear series, the crater changing along the extent of the volcanic fissure. It is enclosed in a circle of lava hills, but far higher than these, and is surrounded by untrod glaciers and dazzling snow-fields ; the earth around seems undermined and footsteps on the plain produce a hollow sound. The cone appeared to us quite regular, the sides at an angle of about 35° ; it is said to have three peaks, the central one the highest. The craters are hollows in the sides, which, with the whole mountain, at the time of our visit, were completely covered with snow; its sides are rent with deep chasms, and numerous cones stud the plain, attesting the great violence of its action.

There is no record of its eruptions before the tenth century; but their number has been twenty-five, with an average interval of thirty-five years, the shortest being six and the longest eighty years. The eruption of 1766 was very violent; after a remarkably mild winter, it began in April to pour out sand, stones, and pumice, some of the latter, six feet in circumference, having been thrown fifteen miles; the sand was carried by the wind to the north-west, covering the land one hundred miles around four inches deep, impeding the boats along the coast, and at noonday making it dark as night; at noon the wind changed to south-east, conveying it to the central desert, or the pastures in the west part of the island would have been entirely destroyed. The lava began to flow in five days, extending five miles to the south-west, and the ejection of water, sand, and stones, with loud reports, did not cease till July. Around it was a fertile plain, buried by this eruption under lava, cinders, and ashes, for an extent of ten miles; the ruins of the houses tell of the fearful destruction at this time, the streams not being confined to the mountain, but ejected from many smaller openings in the plain at its base.

The last eruption was in 1845, which was also preceded by a very mild winter, perhaps from the intensity of the fiery action beneath. It began September 2, with great darkness, showers of stones, sand, and ashes, and loud smothered reports heard many miles away. The ashes were conveyed by the wind as far as the Orkneys, more than six hundred miles. The eruption lasted, with occasional intervals, seven months; the lava streams, though very large, committed no devastation, as most of their course was over a region uninhabited from previous desolation from the same source. There were five craters along the ridge, three large and two small, the former being about three hundred feet deep.

Madame Pfeiffer found the ascent rough and difficult, and it was none the less so fifteen years afterward; and, having surmounted it, she saw nothing but an immeasurable chaos of black lava and dazzling snow, whose contrast was very painful to the eyes. All agree that there is no summit crater, the lava having flowed from the great fissures on the sides, as if the honeycombed rock could not support a column of heavy lava five thousand feet in height. On account of the clouds which surround it, a good view is rare; and most travellers would think it hardly worth while to undergo the fatigue merely to see a scene of desolation, however extensive, — a lifeless panorama of lava, glaciers, lakes, and rivers, with no trace of the works of man.

Captain Forbes, in 1859, found it difficult of ascent, from the sharp masses at the base, the snow and ice

higher up, the steepness of the ledges, and the loose
materials on their sides. He ascended the middle or
highest cone, which is about one-fourth of a mile in
length in a north-east and south-west direction, and
eighty yards across. Happening to ascend on a clear
day, he enjoyed a most extensive view : including
the geysers in the north-west, the glittering blue icy
domes of the jokuls to the north, the terrible Skaptar
to the north-east, and the interminable and untrodden
icy regions beyond ; to the south the blue ocean, and
the Westmann Islands, fifty miles distant ; to the west
the dark cliffs of Thingvalla, — as he says, " the whole
forming a panoramic view unsurpassed, either for interest or beauty, being one of the most extensive and
varied of any in the world."

Attention has recently been drawn, by the terrific
eruption of 1874–75, to the Vatna or Klofa jokul, in
the south-east of Iceland. This comprises a vast
assemblage of mountains, covered with eternal snows,
whose glaciers discharge themselves into the sea on
the south ; the region is about one hundred and fifteen
miles long and sixty miles wide. This great district
of volcano and snow is surrounded by high mountains, among which are the Hofs, Oræfa, and Skaptar
jokuls, — a nest of slumbering monsters, the centres
of terrible eruptions. The northern fringe is hardly
known, as it meets the immense tract of " Odatha-

hraun," the "horrid lava," of about six thousand
square miles, between two great rivers flowing north,
and extending to Lake Myvatn on the north ; in this
black stony sea rise up island-like mountains, whence
the lava has proceeded. To the west are the great
sand deserts, destitute of vegetation ; and to the east,
also, dreary barren wastes, with here and there a
patch of grass. The region is almost unknown, but
is believed to contain, in its northern portion, several
volcanoes always moderately active, and many more
in the southern portions paroxysmal and extremely
violent, from which the last eruption has principally
proceeded.

From the London papers it appears that the eruption began at Christmas, though for seven weeks
before the people had been alarmed by subterranean
noises like thunder extending through more than half
of the island. Early in January followed earthquakes
in all directions, and at last an old extinct volcano
near Vatnajokul opened, and for four weeks continued to eject immense quantities of lava, ashes, and
a muddy fluid mass at boiling heat. The village and
hamlets and farms within a radius of twenty miles
were destroyed, and over a thousand people had to
flee for their lives. After four weeks this volcano
ceased, but at the same time another extinct volcano,
nearly a hundred miles away, near Myvatn, sent its

burning mass upon the country around. This eruption lasted for several weeks, the village of Myvatn
was destroyed, and the whole region for more than
fifty miles around was devastated. More than eight
hundred of the people are reported as having been
rendered homeless. Early in March there seemed to
be a general upheaval of the earth in the whole central portion of the island; new mounds, as it were,
rose to the surface, some to a height of several hundred feet, and over a thousand feet in diameter at the
base, amid tremendous shocks of thundering beneath.
They split open at the top and vomited forth their
burning contents upon the surface around them, covering a distance of two hundred miles. Ten thousand
people are said to have lost nearly all their possessions, and the remainder, who live nearer to and
along the coasts, are themselves too poor to support
such a vast number of needy people. Several hundred persons are also reported to have perished.
The world-renowned Geysers are said to have dried
up since the terrible eruption began, and, instead of
water, to emit immense quantities of hot smoke and
ashes, which, during the night, rising very high into
the air, appear like gigantic columns of flameless fire,
visible for hundreds of miles. It is said that no historic record of any volcanic eruption anywhere in the
world compares with this, either in territory over

12

which it extends, the number of newly-opened craters, or the time of its duration. The Copenhagen Government has issued an appeal for aid to the sufferers.

Another report says, speaking of the eruption in the neighborhood of Myvatn, that on the second of February columns of fire, lava, and stones were shot straight up into the air to a great height and fell back into the crater, or in so narrow a circumference outside it that the formation of new lava only extended twelve miles from north-west to south-east. From the sides of the ravine, at a point as near as they could get from the burning lava, members of an exploring party could see down through the volcanic fissures the lurid flames, like rivers of fire, rushing in wild confusion.

To show the distance to which volcanic materials may be carried by the wind, it is stated that on the morning of the 30th of March, the west coast of Norway, up to the Swedish border, was found covered with a pretty thick layer of dust, which had fallen during the previous night. It lay so thick that less than a pint of snow scraped together and put into a glass to melt, left a tablespoonful of the atmospheric precipitate. Under the microscope, this dust appeared as irregular, small grained and sharp-cornered ashes, for the greater part colorless, but some pieces had a

brownish tinge. Under chemical treatment it turned
out to be a combination of silicates, the bases of the
compound varying. Lime, iron, and alumina were
extracted by treatment with acids. Professor Waage
at once declared that the precipitate must be ashes
from some volcanic eruption carried across to Norway, probably from Iceland.

Professor Magnusson, sub-librarian of the University of Cambridge, England, a native of Iceland, and
our companion to the " Millennial Celebration," wrote
a letter to the " London Times " on this subject, from
which the following are extracts, showing the duty of
Denmark, Great Britain, and, perhaps, of America, in
this great misfortune which has befallen his countrymen : —

" Iceland has this year been visited by a calamity in the
shape of a volcano eruption (in character and extent almost
identical with that of 1783, which proved the death of
fourteen thousand human beings), the inevitable consequences of which will be famine and destruction of human
life on a large scale, unless timely aid should be forth-
coming. A large number of the most prosperous country
districts in the island was laid waste in the course of four
hours last Easter Monday, by being covered with scoriaceous sand, pumice, and volcanic ashes. The inhabitants
have had to fly for life, with their stock, into districts
not yet affected, the pastures of which have been chari-
tably placed at their disposal by the respective owners ;

but, being many times over-stocked, they are beginning already to yield only famishing sustenance. In private letters which I have just received from the distressed parts, it is calculated that pastures to the extent of from two thousand five hundred to three thousand square miles have been destroyed, which supplied the necessary food for forty thousand sheep, two thousand cattle, and three thousand horses. The spread of the distress into those very districts, whose charity is supporting the first sufferers, is itself increasing the evil to an alarming extent ; so that any aid, to be effectual, must make provision, not only for the instant wants of the people, but also for the ensuing winter, as all prospect of a hay harvest (the only harvest known in Iceland) is gone for this year in the immediately affected districts, and is largely impaired in the invaded ones. Food and fodder being immediately required for the starving herds, it is proposed, should this appeal be liberally responded to, as I sincerely hope it will be, to charter a special steamer at the earliest possible date to convey direct to the country, as a first instalment of English charity, such stores as are absolutely necessary at this moment. . . . The unmanured bog lands, which ordinarily yield the hay harvest for cattle, horses, and sheep, are quite useless this year. During May and June, these lands are generally flooded by the rivers which are fed by the waters from the thawing snows on the mountains. The fall of the ashes having covered the snow just before it began to thaw, the waters pouring down from the melting snows have carried with them into these very grass-lands enormous masses of the pumice and the ashes, and deposited them over the lands in so thick a layer that all hope of any hay harvest from them this year is quite out of the question, and it is feared that for years to come the result will be similar. But more than this. The excellent pastures in these parts are principally supplied by the many mountain hollows, small valleys, and other sheltered spots which abound in these mountainous districts, and these are the very places into which the winds have blown the ashes in deep heaps, where they must remain, no one can tell how long, choking the verdure and consequently destroying the pasture for years."

Cattle will have to be slaughtered for want of food, and the consequent increased use of salted meat, and the deprivation of milk, will tend to develop the fearful diseases which follow in the train of scurvy.

Much as the Icelanders love their country, it is difficult to see how, even with prompt assistance from the mother country and still nearer England, many of them will be able to avoid emigration. The proposed American colony may receive large accessions from this catastrophe ; though, from the last accounts, this colonization seems most likely to be beyond the limits of the United States, let us hope that a more genial climate, more fertile soil, and more civilized neighbors, may yet tempt them into our north-western states. We have a plenty of financial, political, and religious earthquakes here, which need give no alarm to an industrious, independent, and thinking people ; and

mother earth is here sufficiently stable for all practical purposes.

Lava, wherever occurring, seems to be of the same
general characters. I have seen the lava of the Sandwich islands, boiling in its fury in the lake at Kilauea,
Hawaii, and have travelled over many a mile of its hardened crust and volcanic sand; and the same appearances I saw in Iceland: the lavas of Vesuvius, Etna,
and Fusiyama, and those from the Philippine islands
and Java do not apparently differ.

There are three kinds described: 1. Smooth, with
a glassy crust, which cools into all imaginable folded
and twisted forms; this is the most common, and
occurs when the flow passes over rocks or dry earth
at a gentle slope, as on the road to the geysers. 2.
Clinkers or scoriaceous lava, rough and fragmentary,
found where the course of the stream has been impeded by obstacles or inequalities of the ground, or
where the heat causes the explosion of caverns in
former flows over which it passes, as seen in the
valley of Thingvalla. 3. The spongy or "horrid"
lava, whose extreme roughness and hardness must be
seen and felt to be appreciated: its jagged mass is
broken into needles, ridges, and crests, like the ice of
a glacier, or the slag of a furnace; this seems to occur
when the lava meets with an impediment which gives
way just as the lava is granulated, rolling the spongy

mass over, and raising huge piles from which the
liquid portion drains away, where it has very suddenly
cooled, or has been broken up after consolidation by
subsequent underground flows. It is not always easy
to draw the line between the last two forms, and, in
Iceland, they generally occur together. The best
idea I can give of the appearance of this rough lava,
is to refer to the piles of dirty snow from the streets
placed on Boston Common during the winter ; after a
day or two of exposure to the sun, the rounded forms
are lost, and jagged and irregular ridges and peaks
make their appearance : if this rough mass could be
at once changed into black lava, one will have, on a
small scale, a tolerably good representation of the last
two varieties, and understand the difficulty and danger
of attempting to pass over them.

Lava is very capricious in its movements — sometimes overwhelming every thing ; at others, turned
aside by slight obstacles — sometimes forming huge
bubbles, which remain as dangerous pitfalls, or as
caverns much used in Iceland for sheepfolds, —
but every where, when recent, black, hard, water-
less, hot from the sun, and indescribably dismal
looking.

This frequent and far-extended series of outpourings
of lava impresses upon the scenery a desolation, barrenness, and blackness, which, in the cold climate of

Iceland, Nature refuses to cover with vegetation; hence the primitive ugliness is in most cases permanent. The country generally looks as if it had been passed out of an infernal laboratory, every thing organic having been burned and boiled out of it, leaving behind an interminable expanse of rough, uninhabitable slag.

It is not to be wondered at, therefore, with the political and commercial disadvantages under which they labor, that the people have little heart to improve their condition ; famine, fire, and pestilence are not calculated for progress. The wonder is that this remnant of the Norsemen have saved themselves from deterioration ; and that they have even stood still for centuries, in face of such terrible elemental foes, preserving their physical vigor, mental independence, and love of country, is a historic marvel.

Iceland is probably situated over the line of a long fissure in the earth's crust, or series of fissures, extending from Jan Meyen to St. Helena, this being, as before stated, evidently the line of volcanic energy.

From whatever source the heat be derived, the action of the sea has greatly modified the ejected lavas, which, on their appearance above the water, have been much changed by glaciers and the floods resulting from their sudden melting. The fiords thus caused afford some very fine and wild scenery, and the lava-bound shores have been shaped by the waves into the most rugged and fantastic forms.

There are four principal theories of the cause of volcanoes, as follows: —

1. The oldest and most natural explanation was that the molten contents of the interior of the earth in this way escaped; the volcano being a kind of safety-valve which prevented too great a laceration of the thin, inhabited crust over the fiery centre. The phenomena of boiling and mineral springs, the escape of heated gases, and the gradual increase of temperature of 1° Fahr. for every sixty feet or thereabouts of descent below the surface, seemed to confirm this view. But the recent researches of astronomers, physicists, chemists, and geologists have so shaken this hypothesis, that it may be stated, I think, without exaggeration, that few first-class geologists now believe in the central fluidity of the earth; but rather that the centre is solid, and that solidification of necessity commenced with the centre. There may be heat there, which some also doubt, but a solidity at least that of glass, probably that of steel.

2. The hypothesis of Sir Humphry Davy, of chemical action from oxidation of minerals and inflammable earths and materials, from the action of water. All the hypotheses seem to require the action of water; and it is a singular fact in confirmation of its neces-

sary presence, that volcanoes, in present and past ages, are either along the edge of continents, in the ocean, or in interior basins communicating with an ample supply of water. Chemical action in the majority of such cases would absorb, rather than disengage, heat ; and this, as a complete explanation, may be at once dismissed.

3. Some geologists, without insisting on, and even denying the central fluidity of the earth, have supposed that, from chemical or electrical or other causes, there may be isolated lakes of molten matter within the external crust of the earth. Admitting the minimum thickness of the crust of the earth to be one hundred miles, only one-fortieth of the distance to the centre ; or even placing it at fifty miles, one-eightieth of the earth's radius ; and taking the united height of the highest mountains and the greatest depth of the ocean at five miles each, or ten miles, — it is readily seen how, in a crust of five times that thickness, there might be reservoirs or lakes of molten materials as large as the Mediterranean Sea, communicating externally, and yet form a very insignificant portion of the earth's crust, communicating with no molten centre. This hypothesis, though possible, is not probable.

4. There remains a fourth hypothesis, recently brought prominently forward by Mallet in England,

but really due to Mr. Vose, a New-England geologist; viz., the central nucleus, though comparatively solid, is constantly cooling and shrinking; this leaves a vacant space between the crust and the central cooling nucleus; as the crust shrinks, after the manner of a wizened, too-long-kept apple, it falls in upon the centre. This motion going on at a tremendous scale, in strata whose depth is measured by miles, is transformed into heat, and with such energy and intensity, probably assisted by the action of highly heated and alkaline waters, as to soften and liquefy the most refractory rocks, and by the accompanying gases or steam to eject the molten materials in the form of lava, in the immense volumes and with the prodigious force, of which we have seen ample evidence in Iceland. According to Professor Hunt, this transformation of motion into heat, on this great scale, occurs in the fluid sedimentary deposits, at various depths, between the cooling crust and the hot but solid nucleus.*

Whichever explanation we adopt, many phenomena

---

* This heat would not only soften and chemically change the lower part of these sediments, but the underlying floor of the older crystalline rocks; thus establishing a line of weakness, or of least resistance, in the earth's crust, coincident with that of the great accumulations of sediment. From this it would result that the wrinkling or corrugation of the earth's crust, due to a contracting nucleus, would be determined along the lines of great sedimentation.

as yet are very imperfectly understood ; at any rate, it seems that our volcanoes are small compared to those of former geological periods, when the crust of the earth was thinner and the nucleus hotter than now ; and it may be stated as a fact, consoling to future generations, that the volcanic energy of our planet is declining.

CHAPTER XVII.

GEOLOGY AND MINERALOGY.

LAVA. — PALAGONITE. — TUFA. — BASALT, OR TRAP. — ELEVATION
AND SUBSIDENCE. — ACTION OF ICE. — GLACIERS. — ACTION OF
WATER. — HEIGHTS OF MOUNTAINS. — SURTURBRAND, OR ICE-
LAND LIGNITE. — ORIGIN. — DRIFT WOOD, OR LOCAL FORESTS.
— SUPPOSED FORMER WARMER CLIMATE. — ICELAND SPAR. —
OBSIDIAN. — MINERALS. — SULPHUR.

IT has been before stated that Iceland is entirely of
volcanic origin, and that geologists have described
three different geological formations. The youngest
is the lava formation, comprising whatever is due to
recent volcanic action, — whether lava proper, slag,
sand, or hot springs.

The next oldest formation consists of strata of
palagonite tufa, intersected by dykes of columnar
basalts, trap, and obsidian of more recent age. Wal-
tershausen, who gave the name palagonite from Pala-
gonia in Sicily, where this mineral abounds, thinks
this the oldest formation in Iceland, a submarine lava
or volcanic ashes modified by water ; and Bunsen calls
it the foundation of the island. The former states that
it contains marine shells and skeletons of silicious
infusoria, which the latter regards as showing its pro-

duction in thermal waters; but I cannot see that this is a justifiable deduction, and no traces of such skeletons have been found in specimens examined in England.

Tufa is a mineral substance of loose texture, composed of a fine cement, which, if the chief ingredient, looks like clay or sand-stone; if it contain fragments of other minerals, it resembles a conglomerate. Palagonite tufa consists mainly of this mineral, which is not unlike a brownish resin in appearance. Basalts are firm and crystalline, fine-grained, and generally dark-colored. Most of the volcanic fissures of Iceland are in this tufa, and it covers large portions of the island, where there is no lava, on the eastern, northern, and north-western coasts. In the vicinity of the large jokuls in the interior and to the south, it forms large and steep mountain ridges; it is the rock underlying the lava streams.

According to Paijkull, the material of this tufa consists of old volcanic ashes and sand, mixed often with scoriæ, ejected beneath the sea, and by its waves and currents arranged in strata, forming a hard, stony mass. It is also believed that this substance may be formed in the air by the long-continued action of rivers, wind, and rain, which heap up around the base of the mountains the same materials as are suddenly thrown out by volcanoes.

The oldest formation is the basalt, enclosing the island as with a belt, especially noticeable in the large fiords and deep valleys of the north, north-west, and east ; it is the principal formation of the country, and underlies the others. Its sheets, however, as dykes, have penetrated from below the upper strata, so that alternating beds of basalt and tufa are not uncommon. It is frequently called trap, from the beds forming layers one over the other, like steps (*trappe*, a step), giving a character to the scenery entirely different from that where the tufas or lavas prevail.

Paijkull places the age of the basalt of Iceland in the latter part of the tertiary epoch, from the fossil plants contained in it. During the post-tertiary or glacier period, the northern continents were enveloped in ice, and some of the lavás of the island are referred to this time ; and the palagonite, between the two, must have been formed toward the close of the tertiary, or the beginning of the post-tertiary period.

As showing the elevation and subsidence of the land, Chambers alludes to what he calls "alluvial terraces," near Reykjavik, — one a hundred, the other thirty feet above the sea ; they were composed of a black dust, the detritus of the rocks. " In this case, the land had at one time been submerged to the depth of the upper terrace, and the valley was an estuary. The river having brought in and laid down a bed of alluvial matter, an uprise at length takes place, leaving that in the open air. The river flows over it, cuts it down, leaving terraces at the sides, and then a new alluvial sheet is spread out in the receded estuary. Another uprise taking place, so as to throw back the sea to where it now is, the second set of terraces is formed in the same way." Perhaps the action of ice and water, in this as in other cases, may afford as good an explanation as the above theory of elevation and subsidence.

The evidences of ice action are numerous in Iceland ; on the road from the capital to Thingvalla the country bears the marks of ancient glacial action, in the shape of rounded eminences (*roches montonneés*), furrowed and striated surfaces, and boulder blocks transported from a distance. Though granite does not exist *in situ* in Iceland, the statement of travellers that they have seen granite boulders there may well be true, this material having been transported from Greenland and the north by the immense sheet of ice which covered the northern hemispheres during the glacial period. Ice has been a mighty agent in making the fiords on the coast, in dredging out the channels about the island, and even in shaping the coast and contour of the Faroe islands. The extent

of the fields of ice around Iceland in modern times
may be understood from the fact, that a field covering
several thousand square miles of the sea north of
Iceland and on the east coast of Greenland, most of
which it is believed had not been moved for four
hundred years, suddenly broke up in 1817; this led
to the famous expedition of Captain Ross, the second
in this century, in search of a north-west passage.
Fields have been since seen covering several hundreds
of square miles. From these facts, the occurrence of
the mammoth in Iceland, of which Dr. Hjaltalin
assured me, is altogether probable ; as the polar bear
in modern times has not unfrequently been carried
to Iceland on ice floes, the mammoth may well have
been transported from Greenland and Siberia on the
ice and glaciers of the post-tertiary age. Some of the
glaciers now existing in Iceland are several hundred
square miles in extent, covering in their slow but
irresistible progress plains formerly fertile and well
inhabited, though now desolate from the combined
action of the fire, ice, and water of the jokuls.

Iceland is the best country in the world for the
study of effects of deluges of water, and their compari-
son with similar older geological phenomena. In the
words of an English geologist : " Carrying with them
disintegrated portions of the rocks and soils over
which they have passed, from the finest mud to the

most enormous rock-fragments, as well as gigantic icebergs, they have deposited the mud, sand, and gravel over great extents of country, frequently as breccias and conglomerates. Sandy wastes and marshes have sprung into existence ; old rivers have been filled up, and new ones, as well as lakes, formed ; miles added to the coast line from encroachments on the sea ; the rocky sides of valleys grooved and scratched and polished by the rocky flood, and the soft sides of mountains washed or rubbed away bodily ; while whole hills of gravel, or other material, have been elsewhere deposited."

The following are the heights of the six principal mountains, measured by Gunnlaugsson : —

Orœfa, 6,241 feet ; ascended by Paulsen in 1794.

Eya-fjalla, 5,432 feet ; never ascended.

Herdubreid, 5,290 feet ; never ascended.

Snæfell, north-east of the Vatna jokul, about 6,808 feet ; never ascended.

Hecla, not quite 5,000 feet, whose summits have often been ascended.

Snæfell's jokul, in the west, seen from Reykjavik, about 4,577 feet, often attempted, but never entirely successfully : by Sir John Stanley in 1789 ; Sir Henry Holland and Dr. Bright, about thirty years after, came very near the summit ; Henderson in 1814, and Captain Forbes in 1859, both failed to reach it. There are several other jokuls, entirely unexplored, on the borders of the lava desert, which are also of great height.

The tufa strata contain a kind of coal or lignite, called "surturbrand," which is of considerable geological interest, though as a source of national wealth of not much importance, as the small supply occurs usually high up in almost inaccessible mountains. It is sometimes seen in the sides of ravines laid bare by torrents, in layers three or four inches thick, composed of very thin plates ; imbedded in it are stems of trees, flattened, more or less carbonized, and cutting like wood ; the interior is as black as ebony, and is sometimes worked in the same way as this wood. Above it is a browner material like burned clay, and over this deposits of loose slag and cinders.

Von Troil, in his letters on Iceland, 1780, says it "is evidently wood, not quite petrified, but indurated, which drops asunder as soon as it comes into the air, but keeps well in water, and never rots ; it gives a bright, though weak flame, and a great deal of heat, and yields a sourish though not unwholesome smell. The Icelanders make a powder of it, which they make use of to preserve their clothes from moths ; they likewise apply it externally against the colick. I have seen tea-cups, plates, &c., in Copenhagen made of surturbrand, which takes a fine polish-

It is found in many parts of Iceland, generally in the mountains in horizontal beds."

The stems are surrounded by branches, roots, and knots, and numerous delicate impressions of leaves, resembling those of the poplar, willow, and birch. The alternation of surturbrand and basalt, the existence of leaves, and the absence of marine shells, show either that all the basalt is not a submarine formation, or, which is most probable, that there have been many depressions and elevations of the surface. Though Olafsen noticed them at the close of the last century, Professor Steenstrup first directed scientific attention thereto ; the remains of the leaves and fruits belong to trees not found in Iceland, but resemble those which formerly grew in tropical America, according to Paijkull, of species now extinct. Beside the trees named, he mentions pines, alder, hazel, oak, elm, plane, vine, tulip, walnut ; in all, about thirty species.

There are two opposite opinions in regard to the origin of surturbrand. According to one, it is derived from old drift-wood, of which the southern coast has at the present time a large amount, brought by the gulf stream from America, and cast ashore by the storms, — a very fortunate circumstance for the people of this treeless country. That this wood comes from temperate, even sub-tropical, waters is proved by the borings of the ship worm (*teredo navalis*). The an cient drift-wood was overwhelmed by depositions, and by heat and pressure converted into coal; the impressions of the leaves are, on this supposition, accounted for by the wood having been imbedded in ice.

According to the other opinion, the surturbrand is derived from stratified forests buried by submarine volcanic eruptions. Some of it, perhaps, may be thus accounted for, but there seems to be no strong evidence that trees of the size and species found ever grew in Iceland. Under either supposition, there must have been great oscillations of the strata. Hooker, in his "Journal of a Tour in Iceland in the Summer of 1809," writes as follows: "In one of these morasses, I passed a woman, driving a horse loaded with the trunk of a tree, which had been dug up close by; it was so large as to appear nearly as great a burthen as the beast could well walk under, and was, probably, five or six feet long, and nearly a foot in diameter." It is dug up in places where not even a bush is seen at present.

Supposing that under a warmer climate, which probably prevailed in Iceland in the intervals of the several glacial periods, there was formerly a luxuriant growth of vegetable matter in these regions, we can understand how it might become covered with an impermeable clay, and thus, the gases being imprisoned, be converted into surturbrand or lignite, stopping short of coal owing to circumstances unfavorable to its production. Dr. Hjaltalin, however, has shown me very good specimens of tertiary bituminous coal.

The delicate nature of the vegetable remains whose impressions have been found seems to forbid the supposition that they could have been conveyed any great distance, and the inference is natural that they grew on the spot. The stems found frequently retain their covering of bark, which is absent in the drift-wood.

Paijkull favors the drift theory, saying that in the gulf stream, in the open sea, delicate leaves and fruits might drift without being knocked about, especially as during the process of decomposition they would float in mid-water, below surface agitation, before sinking to the bottom; in this way, they might be carried hundreds of miles without much injury. " From this point of view," he says, "surturbrand does not testify to the existence of a forest vegetation in Iceland in former ages, but only affords another proof that the Icelandic basalts were formed under the surface of the sea."

Two layers have been found separated by a vein of trap, in a bed of tufa, above which was a stratum of columnar basalt, and fifteen hundred feet above the sea.

In mineralogy Iceland is very rich. The famous double-refracting Iceland spar is now rarely found, and chiefly in ravines on the north and north-east coast, where its narrow seams have been laid bare by the torrents, or broken up by the frosts. Zeolite minerals, calcedonies, and jaspers abound. Obsidian or Icelandic agate, a kind of volcanic glass, opaque and shining black, is abundant ; and near the mud volcanoes of Krabla, in the north, is the remarkable obsidian mountain. Copper and iron, and, it is believed, silver and gold occur, but not in sufficient quantities to be worth working.

The only mineral which can ever form an object of commerce in Iceland is sulphur. This is found in several places, but the most noted and productive mines are near Husavik and the Myvatn lake in the north, and at Krisuvik in the south. The sulphur springs are of two kinds, — hot, gaseous exhalations from the earth, depositing the sulphur, and boiling mud springs. Owing to the difficulty of transportation, the absence of fuel, and the limited amount of the material, it can probably never be a source of national, hardly even of individual, wealth, and can never compete in the markets of the world with the sulphur from Sicily ; should, however, the supply from the latter source be cut off, it might repay the English capitalist to develop the sulphur springs of Iceland.

CHAPTER XVIII.

ICELANDERS IN AMERICA.

"It would be a sad commemoration of the thousandth anniversary of the settlement of the island, if its inhabitants were on that occasion to come to the conclusion that the only future for them was to leave the land where they have now been settled a thousand years. There is, however, no reason to suppose that they will come to such a conclusion, and there is no absolute necessity for such a course."

IN addition to what has been said on the Icelandic exodus, in a previous chapter, a few words kindly sent me by Professor Anderson, of Madison, Wisconsin, will, I think, be interesting, inasmuch as they are reliable; I give them nearly as written in his letter to me.

Icelandic emigration began about the year 1865, when a small party of Icelanders set out for the southern part of Brazil, South America; another little band went thither in 1873. Adding these two parties together, and counting also the single persons who may have found their way to that country since 1865, the number of Icelanders now living in Brazil may be estimated at about one hundred. As there are no prospects that any more will emigrate to South America, the Icelandic colony in Brazil must, in course of time, die out.

The excitement about Brazil led the Icelanders to think of North America; and in 1870 four persons came from Iceland to the United States, and settled in Wisconsin. They sent encouraging letters back to their native island, and the result is that there are now about seven hundred Icelanders in North America. Of these seven hundred, about four hundred and fifty live in the British possessions (three hundred and eighty in Ontario, and seventy in Nova Scotia), and the rest are scattered in various places in the United States, although the majority of them live in Wisconsin. The largest emigrations took place in 1873. and 1874.

Several efforts have been made to concentrate the Icelandic emigration, and bring the emigrants into one colony. Some have tried to get them to settle in Nova Scotia, others in Ontario, others in Alaska, others in Wisconsin, and again others in Nebraska.

The Alaska plan is perhaps the most remarkable. He believes it originated in the mind of Marston Niles of New York; at any rate, he sent for Mr. Jön Olafsson, an Icelander in Wisconsin, and brought it about that Jön Olafsson, Olafur Olafsson, and Päll

13   s

Bjornsson went in a United States ship to Alaska last fall, for the purpose of exploring the country, and to find out whether it was fit for their settlement. The last two remained in Alaska through the winter, and have now come back to Milwaukee, giving a very *unfavorable* account, and saying they will have nothing more to do with Alaska.

Mr. Jön Olafsson returned to New York in the fall, spending the winter in Washington, trying to get some legislation done for the Alaska settlement. He reported very favorably, wrote a little Icelandic book, which was published by the United States Government, and was intended for distribution in Iceland. In the spring of 1875, without having secured any legislation in favor of his project, he went to Iceland ostensibly with a view of working for emigration to Alaska ; but private information from Iceland is conclusive to the effect that his plans are meeting with no favor.

The colony in Wisconsin is small, consisting of about fifty persons, who have as their Icelandic preacher the Rev. Mr. Thorlaksson. Whether they will remain there or not remains to be seen.

Recently, strenuous efforts have been made to form an Icelandic settlement north of Manitoba, in the north-west territory. A large emigration is looked for, after the recent extensive volcanic eruptions in

Iceland. A few weeks ago, a meeting was held in Milwaukee by several Icelanders, who discussed the feasibility of a proposition made to them by the Canadian government, to settle in this north-west territory. Some of the Icelanders present in Milwaukee had just come back from a visit to Manitoba, and were very much pleased with the country. "From the resolutions they passed," writes Professor Anderson, "I should feel warranted in saying, that it is quite probable that a large Icelandic settlement will be attempted in the Red River Valley, north of Manitoba, and time will have to determine whether the plan is a wise one or not. I have, as yet, no opinion in the matter; but I know many Icelanders are hopeful in regard to it." The plan is to gather all the Icelanders that have emigrated, and may emigrate, to the Red River Valley, where the Canadian government seems to have offered very favorable inducements.

Among Icelanders of some note in Europe may be mentioned: In England and Scotland, Gudbrandr Vigfusson, of Oxford University, editor of Cleasby's Icelandic–English Dictionary; Eirikur Magnusson, of Cambridge University, a member of our party, translator of several Icelandic Sagas; Jön Hjaltalin, of the Advocate's Library, Edinburgh, Scotland, translator of Orkneyinga Saga; S. Sveinbjörnsson, of Edinburgh, a distinguished musician, who composed the "Hymn of Praise" for the millennial festival in Iceland, a piece of music which we heard sung, and which is given in a previous chapter, pages 70–73.

Among the Icelanders who have come to this country, there are six of scholarly attainments. 1. Professor Jön Bjarnason, who was formerly a minister in Reykjavik. He has for the last year been a professor in Luther College, Decorah, Iowa, and is now living with Professor Anderson in Madison, Wisconsin, and they are working together at the Sagas. 2. Päll Thorlaksson, a thorough Icelandic scholar, who is pastor of the Icelanders in Wisconsin. 3. Jön Olafsson, a poet and journalist, who was compelled to leave Iceland on account of his strong republican tendencies. He is the one who went to Alaska, and is now in Iceland. Besides these, there are three who are eminent specimens of self-made men: Olafur Olafsson, Fridjön Fridriksson, and Sigtryggr Jönasson. These are all scholars, well versed in Icelandic, Danish, English, German, and French.

At the same time that we were assisting at the millennial celebration in Iceland, the Norse population in America were not unmindful of this important event. According to Professor Anderson, between sixty and seventy Icelanders assembled in church at Milwaukee on Sunday, Aug. 2, 1874, to hear a sermon on the past and present of Iceland. After church, they marched to a park, where, clad in some respects in their national costume, they listened to patriotic speeches from Jön Olafsson, Olafur Olafsson, Professor Anderson, and other Icelandic scholars; interspersing the addresses with native songs, allusions to and cheers for the friends of Iceland in all countries, especially Jön Sigurdsson, to whom more than to any one else the new Constitution, and whatever glimpses of independence it affords, is due, — a man whom Professor Fiske, the Scandinavian scholar of this country, considers "worthy of being placed by the side of Gladstone, in England, as a scholar and statesman."

The sermon alluded to was by Professor Jön Bjarnason, and the first Icelandic sermon in America on record.

The millennial festival was also appropriately remembered in New York city, Ithaca, and Chicago.

Since the above was written, I have learned that about two hundred and eighty Icelanders have gone to the Red River Valley, and are now there. They will probably call their settlement "Leifsland," in honor of Leif Erikson, who came to America in the year 1000.

CHAPTER XIX.

THE FUTURE OF ICELAND.

POLITICAL AGITATION IN ICELAND. — THE NEW CONSTITUTION,
AND ITS PROVISIONS. — ANALYSIS OF IT. — WHAT IT IS GOOD
FOR. — DISAPPOINTMENT OF THE PEOPLE. — ALLEGORICAL PIC-
TURE OF THE PAST AND PRESENT OF ICELAND. — AUTHOR'S
IMPRESSIONS OF THE PEOPLE. — WHAT IS WANTED FOR THE
FUTURE PROSPERITY OF ICELAND.

> "The law of force is dead!
> The law of love prevails!
> Thor, the Thunderer,
> Shall ride the earth no more.
> Sing no more,
> O ye bards of the North,
> Of Vikings and of Jarls!
> Of the days of old
> Preserve the freedom only,
> Not the deeds of blood."

HAVING briefly sketched the glorious past of Iceland, and given as clear an idea as my space
will allow of its present condition, these pages may
properly be concluded by a short statement of what its
interesting and liberty-loving people may hope for in
the future, and especially what they may expect from
the "new constitution," which was the boon conferred
upon them during the visit of his Danish Majesty.

Since 1845, when some concessions were made to Iceland by Denmark, there has been a persistent agitation to ameliorate the condition of the island, by securing to it a voice in the regulation of its government, and in the appropriation of its revenues at home. The one to whom the country is principally indebted for the present good and the future promise in the "new constitution," is John Sigurdsson, a native, and without doubt the most popular and patriotic man in Iceland, who, unfortunately, was not present to receive the admiring plaudits of his countrymen.

Before giving the new constitution, the reader is informed that it, as well as a condensed statement of its chief points, was translated for the use of the newspaper correspondents of our party, by Professor Magnusson, of Cambridge, England, our native Icelandic companion. The whole document was published in the newspapers at the time, but is here introduced as an interesting chapter of political history, and as showing how hard it is for royalty to yield any thing to the just demands of a people desirous of governing themselves by republican principles.

According to taste, therefore, the reader may take the whole constitution or its abstract, neither of which would have been entirely intelligible without the preceding general information.

THE CONSTITUTION OF ICELAND.

CHAPTER I.

RELATIONS BETWEEN ICELAND AND DENMARK.

ARTICLE 1.· The power of legislation rests with the King and the Althing; executive power with the King alone; judiciary power with the Judges. Iceland has no part in Imperial matters, pays no revenues to Denmark, and has no representation in the Danish Rigsdag.

2. The King governs through a Minister, called Minister for Iceland. He may or may not be a member of the Cabinet. The King appoints the Governor, who receives his orders through the Minister.

3. The Minister can be impeached by the Althing, after forms of law to be enacted hereafter. The Althing may petition the King against acts of the Governor, and the King may order his impeachment at his pleasure, or remove him.

4. All officers appointed by the King must be native-born subjects of Denmark, and must speak the Icelandic language. He may remove an officer or transfer him, but not degrade him to a lower office or salary.

5. The regular Althing is to assemble every second year, and to sit not more than six weeks, except by command of the King. This may be changed by law.

6. The King may call extraordinary sessions, and direct the period of their duration.

7. The King may adjourn the regular Althing, but not over four weeks, unless the Althing consents; not more than once, however, the same year.

8. The King may dissolve the Althing; in which case there shall be new elections within two months, and the newly elected Althing shall be summoned to meet the year following.

9. The King shall have power to lay draughts of bills before the Althing.

10. If the King has not given his assent to a bill within two years, it cannot have the power of law, and is null and void.

11. When the King considers it necessary, he may decree *ad interim* laws. These must not, however, violate the Constitution. They must be laid before the Althing at the next session, though, unless with the assent of the King, they cannot be annulled.

12. All power of reprieve rests with the King.

13. The King may directly, or by royal commission, grant exemption from the operation of laws enacted by the Althing under the new Constitution, in case they conflict with laws formerly in force.

CHAPTER II.

THE CONSTITUTION OF THE ALTHING.

14. The Althing shall consist of thirty-six Deputies ; thirty to be elected by the people, six appointed by the King; the number of the former may be altered by law. The Deputies shall be elected for six years unless the Althing shall be sooner dissolved by the King ; the six appointed by the King, however, in case of dissolution, hold on to the end of the term of their appointment. All of the thirty-six must be Icelanders. If a Deputy dies or resigns, and his place is filled by election, the new Deputy holds office only until the end of the term.

15. The Althing shall consist of two Chambers, the upper comprising twelve, the lower twenty-four members ; these numbers may be altered by law.

16. Those appointed by the King are *ex officio* members of the upper house ; the other six are elected by the entire body,

13*

meeting in general session. If a seat becomes vacant in the upper house, the Althing meets in general session to fill the vacancy, after the district shall have elected a new Deputy.

17. All bondsmen (farmers) who cultivate a grass field and who pay taxes shall have the right of franchise ; special exemptions may, however, be granted by law from paying some particular tax, without forfeit of franchise. All residents of towns who pay a municipal tax of four rix-dollars have the franchise ; also, men of the dry booth, — that is, men who have no cows, milkless men, referring especially to fishermen, — who pay a tax of six dollars a year ; public functionaries, who are appointed either by royal writ or by local authority ; and all who have passed an examination at the University or the Theological Seminary at Reykjavik, or other institutions provided by law, provided they are not so bound as to have the action of their will controlled by others. A voter must be twenty-five years old, have a good character, and must have resided in the district where he votes at least one year ; he must be of sound mind, and without restraint ; he must not be in receipt of support from the poor-law fund, or, having received it, he must have paid it back, or been exempted from so doing by law.

18. Any one in the above five classes may become a Deputy by election to the Althing, provided he is not the subject of another Power, or in its service. He must, however, have resided the last five years of his life in lands subject to Denmark, and have completed his thirtieth year.

CHAPTER III.

DUTIES OF THE ALTHING.

19. The Althing shall meet on the first working day of July every second year, unless the King otherwise orders.

20. The place of meeting shall be Reykjavik, unless on special occasion the King may fix upon another place.

21. Each Chamber of the Althing has the right to draft bills, and to send addresses to the King.

22. Each Chamber may appoint committees to sit during the session of the Althing, to consider matters of public concern, with power to send for persons and papers.

23. All taxes must be regulated by law, and no land shall be taken up or sold except by law.

24. No funds shall be taken from the Treasury, unless provision is made therefor by the general budget or by special law.

25. At the first meeting of the Althing, a budget sufficient for two years shall be laid before the lower Chamber. The income to provide for the expenditure shall be fixed and extraordinary; the latter, according to the relations of Iceland in the realm, as by Act of July 2, 1871, is to be paid out of the general Treasury to Iceland, yet in such way that, before any thing else, shall be paid the salaries of the higher functionaries of the island and the Royal Commissioner at the Althing.

26. Each Chamber has the right to demand an explanation of every item in the budget.

27. No bill shall be passed by either Chamber until it has been discussed three times.

28. When a bill has passed one Chamber, it is sent to the other. If altered, it is returned; if again altered or amended in the Chamber where it originated, it is again sent to the other Chamber, when if not now agreed to, both Chambers meet, and the bill is disposed of in Althing at one discussion. In case of such meeting, two-thirds of the members of each Chamber shall be present, and take part in the voting, a majority ruling on each paragraph. But on every bill, except the budget, the votes of two-thirds of all Deputies present are requisite to its passage

29. The Deputies shall decide upon the legality of elections to the Althing.

30. Immediately on his election being declared valid, the Deputy shall take an oath to obey the Constitution.

31. The Deputies are bound only by their convictions, and are not to receive instructions from the electors after being chosen. Public functionaries elected by the people do not require permission from the government to accept, but they are bound, without expense to the Treasury, to have their official duties attended to in their absence in a manner satisfactory to the government.

32. While the session lasts, no Althing's man may be arrested for debt, without consent of the Chamber in which he has his seat, nor may he be imprisoned nor proceeded against at law, unless taken in the actual commission of crime, nor can he be called to account for words spoken in the Althing, unless with consent of the Chamber.

33. If any Deputy lawfully elected shall violate the provision of the Constitution which makes him ineligible, he violates his privileges as a Deputy.

34. The Governor shall have the right to a seat in the Althing and to take part in the debate, under the rules of the Houses. The government may also give permission to another man to sit, and, on demand, deliver to the Althing all official documents and reports which may be required. The Governor has only the right to vote when he may be at the same time a legally elected Deputy.

35. Each Chamber elects its President or Speaker — a Deputy ; also the general Althing when together.

36. Neither Chamber shall discuss any measure, unless two-thirds of its members are present.

37. No Deputy shall make any proposal without permission of the Chamber.

38. No measure shall be considered unless a Deputy shall be responsible for its introduction.

39. If the Chamber cannot decide a question, they may refer it to the Governor.

40. The sittings of both Chambers shall be open to the public, yet on certain occasions discussions may be secret.

41. Rules for the sittings of the collected Althing shall be fixed by law.

CHAPTER IV.

THE JUDICIARY.

42. The formation of the judiciary shall be fixed by law.

43. The Judges shall decide the sphere of public functionaries when appealed to.

44. Judges can only proceed in accordance with law. A Judge cannot be deprived of the magisterial functions, without judgment of the other Judges ; and no Judge can be transferred to any other office against his will, unless his affairs be mismanaged. At the age of sixty-five he may resign, without losing his salary.

CHAPTER V.

RELIGION.

45. The Evangelical Lutheran Church shall be the national Church, and the State shall assist it as such.

46. The people shall have the right to form societies for the worship of God according to their consciences, so long as they respect good morals and public order.

47. No one shall forfeit his national rights on account of religion, nor can he excuse himself on that account from public duties.

CHAPTER VI.

RIGHTS OF THE CITIZEN.

48. Any person suspected of crime, and held as such, shall be taken before a magistrate as soon as possible. If he cannot be discharged immediately the Judge shall give his decision in

three days as to whether he is to be committed for trial. If he be discharged on bail, the Judge shall fix it. A decision in either case may be appealed to a higher authority. No person can be imprisoned for a misdemeanor which by law is punishable by fine.

49. The house of the citizen shall be sacred. No domicile shall be invaded, nor any documents or letters stopped or opened, except upon the order of a law court, unless the law shall provide a special exception.

50. The right of property shall be sacred. No person shall be required to give up his property, except for the public good, and then only by special law, which shall at the same time grant full restitution.

51. Every man shall have the right to work at his trade, without interference by the law or by other citizens.

52. He who cannot support himself and family shall have the right of support from the common poor-law fund, and in return shall perform such duties as the law requires.

53. If parents have not the means to educate their children, or if the children are orphans or paupers, it shall be the duty of the public to educate and bring them up.

54. Freedom of the press is absolute. There shall be no censorship, and the man shall be responsible to the courts of law for his utterances in case of libel.

55. The people shall have the right to organize societies, without leave of government, and the government cannot dissolve a society : yet they may be prosecuted at law, and dissolved by the decision of a court.

56. The people have the right to meet in public, without weapons. The police have the right to attend all public meetings. Public meetings may only be forbidden when they are likely to disturb the public peace.

57. Every able-bodied citizen shall be required to defend the land in case of invasion.

58. The rights of communities to regulate their own affairs under the supervision of government shall be regulated by law.

59. All affairs concerning taxation shall be settled by law.

60. All special rights which the law has attached to nobility, title, and dignities shall be annulled.

CHAPTER VII.

AMENDMENTS TO THE CONSTITUTION.

61. Amendments to the Constitution may be proposed either in a regular or an extraordinary Althing. If the proposal pass the lower Chamber, the Althing shall at once dissolve, and new elections shall take place. If the new Althing approve, the amendment or alteration is adopted.

62. This Constitution comes into force on the 1st of August, 1874.

Of its seven chapters, the first states the relation between the king and the Danish government, on the one hand, and the Althing, or Icelandic assembly, on the other. The legislative power belongs to the king and Althing: the executive power to the king alone; and the judicial power to the judges. Iceland has no voice in Danish national questions, is not represented in the Rigsdag at Copenhagen, and pays nothing of the national expenditures; nor does she wish to. The highest power in Iceland is the Governor appointed by the king, any complaints of the Althing being decided by the king, who would naturally lean towards his officer; this clause practically amounts to nothing against any oppression of the people, for the minister for Iceland, to whom the governor is responsible, is overruled by the king. The Althing, convened by the king, sits for six weeks only, every other year ; there is no necessity, and no pecuniary or political inducement, as with us, to prolong the session as long as possible ; he may, however, prolong the session, call special ones, and dissolve it at his pleasure ; and no bill becomes a law unless signed by him : so that the powers of the Althing, as we understand political matters, do not amount to much either for public or private good.

Other chapters define the constitution and functions of the Althing, which consists of thirty deputies chosen by the people, holding office for six years, and six appointed by the king, retaining their places if the Althing be dissolved. There are two houses : the upper consisting of the six deputies appointed by the king and six chosen by the thirty out of their number ; the lower house consists of the other twenty-four elected deputies. The usual parliamentary laws govern the proceedings ; this body, though it has the control, by a biennial budget, of the finances of the island, must see to it that the salaries of Danish officials and deputies take precedence of all other expenditures. In addition to this provision for " number one," Denmark has the power to prevent any disagreeable legislation ; for, as two-thirds of the

members of either house constitute a quorum, if five
of the king's deputies stay away legislation by the
concurrent action of the two houses is impossible, —
a provision which cannot be said to grant much freedom of self-government.

It is no exaggeration to say that the professions of
the power of self-government made in this "new constitution" amount to little or nothing; as the royal
prerogative opportunely steps in when there is any
danger of additional liberty. It was perfectly well
understood by the people as illiberal, almost despotic,
though some demagogues chose to see in it a Magna
Charta; they accept it, however, as the best they can
get, and especially as being the beginning of a political education, which, in course of time, will enable
them to demand and to obtain political independence.

In the words of Mr. Taylor: "The great service
which Jön Sigurdsson has rendered to Iceland is not
so much in the gift of this constitution as in the fact
that he has broken the long apathy of the people,
persuaded them to ask, and secured them a result
which means courage for the future, if not satisfaction with the present. In this sense, the 1st of
August, 1874, is the opening of a new era in Iceland's history."

Before concluding this chapter on the future of
Iceland, I wish to allude to a picture made in com-

T

memoration of the Millennial Celebration, and sold thereat, which comprises in a small compass much of the history of the country, and will serve as a reminder of its chief characteristics.

The picture represents a stone archway with two pillars. In the centre is seen the white cone of an ice mountain towering above the sea, on each side of which, in the leaden sky beyond, are the dates of 874 and 1874, which is the interval of time celebrated. On the top of the jokul is seated the "Lady of the Mountain," or Iceland represented as a female figure, holding in her left hand a roll of parchment, and with her right leaning on a sword, her face turned toward the glorious past; on her right shoulder is sitting one of the ravens of Odin, that every morning gave him tidings of all that was going on; her head is wreathed with ice crystals and flames of fire, the two antagonistic elements of the island. On the Mountain beneath her feet is a Latin inscription which has been thus translated by an Icelandic scholar : —

"Ten centuries thou sawest fade, patient, still unvanquished Thule ;
    Glorious mother, may God grant thee life of thousand centuries !
    We pray that God Almighty may crown thee with freedom,
    And deliver thee from evil, after thy woes are ended."

In the middle of the space below, supposed to be the ocean, is a map of Iceland, surrounded by the four protecting genii of the land, represented after Snorre

Sturleson's record in the "Heimskringla," in which he tells us that, owing to the maltreatment by king Harald, of some Icelanders on the coast of Denmark, the indignant islanders sent him word that they intended by way of reprisal to make as many lampoons on him as there were noses (or heads) in Iceland. So dreaded were these sharp satires that the king proposed to sail to Iceland to avenge this scornful mockery. According to one of the sagas, the king ordered one of his magicians to go thither in the shape of a whale and reconnoitre. Going to the west coast he found all the mountains full of genii, great and small, and when he tried to land in one of the fiords a huge dragon rushed toward him, with a train of serpents and toads, that blew poison upon him ; turning into another fiord a bird flew against him, so large that its wings stretched across the mountains ; going south, a large gray bull attacked him, wading into the sea, and bellowing frightfully ; at Rejkianess there came down the hill a giant, higher than the mountains, with an iron staff in his hands, and many other giants following him. Thus baffled at every point, he swam along the coast, finding nothing but barren sand and deserts, dangerous rocks, and a wide expanse of stormy ocean. The king concluded, on the return of his messenger, that he would not undertake the voyage.

These saga myths represent, in a manner, the natural phenomena of Iceland, — the dragon and the giant represent the subterranean agencies of the volcano and the geyser, the bird the sharpness of the frost and the brightness of the ice, and the bull the roaring ocean, — and they are placed accordingly at the four corners of the island.

Around the map of the island is the first stanza of the popular Icelandic national song written by their eminent lyric poet, Bjarne Thorarensen (who died in 1841), translated thus : " World-old Iceland, beloved foster-land, thou wilt be loved by thy sons as long as the ocean girds the lands, men love women, and the sun shines on mountains." On the right higher up is typified the discovery of Greenland by the Icelander, Erik, the Red, in 982 ; and on the left, of America, or Vinland, by Leif, the Lucky, in 1000 ; and between them are the symbols of the achievements of Iceland, viz., poetry, science, and warfare, represented by a harp, books, and weapons. Below the map are shown typical views of Iceland, — a jokul, or ice mountain, with a waterfall in the middle, glittering in the rays of the rising sun ; on the left the geyser, on whose column of steam the giant is treading, as an abstraction or myth, without weight or reality ; on the right, Hecla in eruption, toward whose column of smoke the dragon is blowing, emblematic of the volcanic forces.

Below these an Icelandic verse, signifying, "Old, for ever ice-clad land, be to us ever the wonderful sight thou wast to the eyes of thy first settlers."

On the base of the left pillar is the symbol of malignity, biting its own tail; on the base of the right, a Norse galley, signifying the old navigation of Iceland; over these respectively the names of Ingolf and Thorleif, the first settlers. On the shafts are written the names of thirty-two distinguished first settlers; from a vase crowning each shaft rise leafy branches following the arch of the gate, and forming a garland over a female figure; in the middle, and also on the breast of the mountain lady, is the sacred five-rayed star of heathenism. On the leaves of the garland, and of other branches springing from the vase, are inscribed the names of such Icelanders as have distinguished themselves in their country's history, one hundred and forty-two in number, only two of whom are living — one, the patriot, Jön Sigurdsson; the other, Bjorn Gunnlaugsson, an eminent geographer and mathematician, now eighty-six years old.

In the top of each branch,* on each side of the name Island (Iceland), perches an eagle, a bird which, according to their sagas, "knoweth many things;" and, lastly, under each corner of the name, an Icelandic and a Latin inscription, meaning "in commemoration of the colonization of Iceland, one thousand years ago."

---

* The world-tree Yggdrasil.

This embodies at a glance the glorious deeds and history of Iceland ; its discoveries, the myths of its sagas, and the characters of its scenery, and is, in fact, an epitome of what was celebrated at their Millennial Anniversary in 1874. Made by Benedikt Groudal.

Finally, my impression of this people, grave and inexpressive like the cold sons of the north, was that they are born republicans ; while asking from the king of Denmark a new constitution, granting them the privilege of self-government, they would pay no part of the expenses of that kingdom, and take no share in its government ; yielding to the sovereign only that re-spect which they demanded from him. All they asked was a certain degree of political independence, and especially to impose their own taxes, and apply them to the development of the intellectual and material interests of the island as they think proper. The new constitution, though, in most respects, a " glitter-ing generality," high-sounding words without practical concession of greater freedom, was accepted by the people as a beginning, the shadow of a substance in the future. Such concession on the part of Denmark alone can remove their national hatred of the mother country. This, or at least a national indifference, was everywhere manifest during the recent visit of the king ; the coldness of his reception was so evident that it must have wounded him, as, in his kindness of heart, he certainly wished to do something for the benefit of Iceland; he doubtless thought he had, but the keen scalpels of these republicans soon pierced the thin wordy covering of the long-drawn sentences, and came down to the hard skeleton of the old familiar despotism; they asked for bread, and they got a stone. The people looked upon the pageant, and said nothing; they even scorned, in their national pride, to use any language but the Icelandic, even when they understood Danish. There was little enthusiasm, except among the Danes, a few officials, and the aspiring demagogues who are found there, as elsewhere, ready to bend the knee to kingly power.

What Iceland especially wants are better means of communication than the small uncomfortable steamers which now make about eight trips a year; foreign capital to develop their fisheries and mineral wealth, and improve their breeds of sheep, horses, and cattle; larger and better boats and tackle; the making of roads and deepening of harbors; with better accommodations for the summer tourists who would be glad to visit its magnificent and peculiar scenery; and, at the present time, the sympathy and assistance of other nations to enable the people to recover from the recent volcanic eruption which has devastated the south-eastern portion of the island.

While we may not agree with Mr. Babbage, that their mighty volcanic agents and glaciers may be converted into useful instruments of human industry, we may believe that these may cease to be destructive; that their literature may receive the attention from scholars and antiquarians that it merits; that new avenues of trade and increased production may prevent famines; that attention to the laws of health, securing pure air, cleanliness, and nourishing food, may cause desolating epidemics to cease; and that with the privileges asked for, and to a small extent granted, in the new constitution, Iceland may regain and maintain her place in the family of nations.

She is like her own twilight: her sun has set, but the splendor of her bright historic day illuminates her during her night of oppression and apathy, — to be again a shining light, let us hope, under the influence of her rising independence.

And now, I trust that the reader will admit that Iceland was justified in proclaiming to the nations the celebration of her thousandth anniversary; that she deserves the admiration of the civilized world for what she has done for liberty, the advance of knowledge, and the preservation of historic records, at a time when the rest of Europe was in darkness; and especially that she has proved that man is superior to his surroundings, and that hardship, oppression, and poverty can neither stifle the aspirations for liberty, nor degrade a poetic and heroic race.

May we not say, with Milton : " Methinks I see a noble nation, rousing herself like a strong man after sleep; methinks I see her as an eagle, renewing her mighty youth, and kindling her endazzled eyes at the full mid-day beam."

14

CHAPTER XX.

USEFUL INFORMATION.

WHAT THERE IS TO SEE IN ICELAND. — USEFUL INFORMATION
FOR TRAVELLERS. — WHERE AND HOW TO START. — CLOTHING,
TENT, AND FOOD. — EXPENSES AND MONEY. — WHO SHOULD
GO TO ICELAND.

> " Now Neptune's month our sky deforms,
> The angry night-cloud teems with storms ;
> And savage winds, infuriate driven,
> Fly howling in the face of heaven ! "

IT has been before mentioned that we started from
Iceland for Scotland in a heavy sea, and that our
voyage homeward was of the roughest character, not
unattended by danger, and with many bodily discomforts. The inquiry naturally arises, what is there in
this remote island, surrounded by an ocean almost
always stormy, which can tempt a traveller toward it,
out of the way of modern facilities and almost of the
conveniences and necessaries of life.

In the absence of millennial attractions, the future
traveller in Iceland, until 2874, must content himself
with its grand scenery, volcanic phenomena, and
Scandinavian people. There is the grandeur and
desolation of ice and lava, but also the green hue of

vegetation, and a verdure capable of supporting man and his domestic animals ; rich pastures and extensive meadows support a contented but scattered population, almost to the edge of everlasting ice and in close proximity to the slumbering volcano ; the flowers are abundant and beautiful. The fury of the waves on the lava coast ; the precipitous sides of the fiords, washed by the sea ; the icy jokuls on every hand ; the lava deserts, cracked and distorted in the most picturesque manner ; the short and icy rivers ; the placid but dismal lakes ; the hot springs and the geysers ; the basaltic walls of Thingvalla, over which pours a fine cascade ; the views of Hecla, and Snæffels, and the glittering mountains which bound the great desert on the south and west, form a list of things to be seen in Iceland, and nowhere else, in which any enthusiastic traveller would delight. To the mineralogist and geologist it is a land of exceeding interest ; to the sportsman, its salmon, plover, curlew, ducks, and grouse offer tempting inducements.

The point of departure should be the capital, as there guides understanding English, Danish, and Icelandic can readily be obtained. As walking is impossible, principally on account of the rivers and bogs, horses must be hired or bought ; the last is preferable for extended journeys, as they can usually be sold for a fair price at the end of the journey; we found the necessary expenses about the same as when travelling on the continent, — about five dollars per day.

When we consider that the first steamer touched there not more than twenty years ago, it is quite a satisfactory progress to have a regular steamer sailing from Copenhagen, touching at Leith in Scotland, and making six or eight passages each way during the year, from May to October. The fare from Scotland is twenty-five dollars in gold each way, with a small additional expense for the steward.

The traveller requires ordinary winter clothing, woollen undergarments, strong boots, and Mackintosh. I found rubber leggings very serviceable, both against water and mud. He must take his own food with him, and a tent; he will not find any inns, but the clergymen will generally receive him hospitably, offering the comforts of their houses and the protection of their churches, accepting no pay in money, but grateful for any useful present; in pleasant weather he will not care to sleep in the houses, or even the churches, for entomological reasons. A tent seven feet long and five feet high is ample for three persons; it should not weigh more than eighty pounds, or half a load for a horse.

Danish money should be taken, or obtained at the capital, and in small pieces. A Danish "skilling" is

equal to an English farthing, or about half a cent ;
sixteen skillings make a "mark," four and a half-
pence, a little less than nine cents ; six marks make
a "rigsbank dollar," two shillings and threepence, or
fifty cents; two rigsbank dollars make a "specie dollar," four shillings and sixpence, or one American
silver dollar. A pound sterling equals about eight
rigsbank dollars and four marks, taking out the
money-changer's commission.

Ordinary health, love of nature in her wildest
moods, a disposition to make the best of every thing,
and not to be incommoded by tent life, rough fare,
exposure to cold and wet, and not a little fatigue and
discomfort, are prerequisites for travelling in Iceland.
Even ladies have made the trip, though, from my own
experience and that of Madame Pfeiffer, I should not
advise the trial, unless after such familiarity with
mountain and horseback travelling, as the Alps and
the Yosemite valley would give. Whoever goes
under these circumstances will be sorry, I am sure,
as I was, when it is necessary to say " good-by to
Iceland."

NOTES.

Thingvalla.

Page 12, line 1. The Icelandic nominative is in the plural Thingvellir; but the stem is Thingvoll, or in the plural Thing-volls. Thingvalla, though grammatically erroneous, is retained in the text as being the word almost universally known to English readers of Icelandic travels.

Literary Spirit.

Page 40, lines 9–12. This should be modified by the statement that there is a remarkable revival of the old Icelandic literary spirit in the present century, as exhibited by their poets, historians, linguists, and journalists.

Sea-Serpent.

Page 56, line 8. At the meeting referred to, Dr. Hagen said that he had, in 1839, accompanied Professor Rathke in his visit to Norway to collect evidence in regard to the sea-serpent, the reality of which no Norwegian doubts; and Dr. Hagen expressed himself convinced of its existence. I have since learned from Professor Anderson that Professor Sars, of Christiania, a distinguished naturalist, and son of the famous Michael Sars, believes in its existence, and has been fishing for it for some years at public expense. Many people in Norway, and among them the distinguished musician, Ole Bull, declare that they have seen it.

Warm Springs.

Page 67, line 22. About three or four miles from the capital are warm springs, which we could not find, which still emit steam visible from the harbor.

Norwegian Myth.

Page 94, line 21. See pp. 13 and 14 of "Afraja," or, Life and Love in Norway, by Theodore Mügge; translated by Morris, and recently published by Porter and Coates (Philadelphia), where a similar myth is given about the origin of Norway.

Love of Country.

Page 95, line 21. This is said by some to be a mere fabrication, probably of Danish origin, as nothing like it is to be found in Icelandic literature. It is, however, a not uncommon saying, which, if true, would not speak well for the sanity of the people, especially after this year's repetition of the terrible volcanic eruptions which have come from the region of the Vatna jokul.

Uses of Churches.

Page 134, line 1. During the last century, it was the custom in many places to use the churches as storehouses. They are not generally now so used, as it is prohibited by law; and what we saw indicating such use is easily accounted for by exceptional circumstances.

Geysers.

Page 146, last line but 5. Geysers are found most abundantly in the middle portions of Iceland; in many districts they are not found, and rarely, if ever, near the sea.

Danes and Swedes.

Page 162, last line but 4. It is said that only one Dane and very few Swedes were among the *original* settlers in Iceland; at present the Danes are very few, and there are no Swedes.

Kongespeil.

Page 172, line 18. The Icelandic name of this book is *Konungs skuggsjá*, the above name being a Danish translation of the word ; it means " Kings' mirror."

Population and Occupations.

Page 186, line 7. The latest census makes the population of Iceland a little more than seventy thousand, which would change the figures in the text to one and a half and eight respectively. Of this number about five-sevenths are farmers, and of the rest a little more than one-third are fishermen, and the remainder merchants, mechanics, and day laborers.

Saturday.

Page 188, line 2. This day was never called after any Roman god in the north ; it was called " laugardag," which means "washing-day."

Floki's Landing.

Page 204, last line but 5. Recent authorities state that the place where Floki landed was probably Isafjord.

The Althing.

Page 207, line 11. Strictly speaking, Norway had no " Althing," but a " Thing " for each district ; and these " Things " served as models for the formation of the " Althing " in Iceland.

Governor's Term of Service.

Page 215, line 18. I have been recently informed that the time of service as Governor is indefinite, and that it may be for life.

Greenland Settlements.

Page 220, last line. There seems little doubt that the Danish settlements in Greenland were on the west coast.

14*   U

Professor Anderson.

Page 224, line 4. He was born of Scandinavian parents, but in this country ; and therefore calls himself a Norse American.

Columbus.

Page 229, line 6. Professor Anderson has recently suggested that perhaps Columbus might have thought that the Vinland which the Norsemen had found, and which Adam of Bremen wrote about, was the very India to which he wanted to find a western route, and that what he wanted to know was whether land could be reached by sailing westward ; if he ever had such an opinion, he must have have got it confirmed in Iceland. His own belief is that Columbus thought the Icelanders had discovered India ; — see No. 40, Oct. 7, 1875, of the " Christian at Work," where he has an article on the discovery of America.

The Sagas and Edda.

Page 233, line 8. The sagas, properly so called, though poetic in their style, were written in prose. Snorre's Edda treats of mythology in prose, and the Heimskringla of the Scandinavian and other continental nations ; the first has been translated into English by Dasent, and the latter by Samuel Laing. The " Landnamabok " may be compared to " Doomsday Book " in England.

Icelandic Schools.

Page 244, line 14. Medicine and theology are now studied in Reykjavik ; many of the students of the latter we came across in our travels, and very pleasant companions they were. Our good friend Dr. Hjaltalin is president of the medical school ; there is as yet no law school at home.

Donations of Books.

Page 245, line 20. The books all arrived, but not so soon as expected ; and a catalogue of them has been published in Iceland.

Great Eruption of 1875.

Page 269, line 15. The following are extracts from a letter to me from Dr. Jön Hjaltalin, of Reykjavik, dated Aug. 31, 1875 : —

" Since one of our largest volcanoes, Kötlugia, situated on the eastern flank of Myrdalsjokul, made its last eruption in 1860–61, we have had no subterranean disturbances of any serious nature until the beginning of this year, and especially since spring ; when in April a great volcanic eruption took place from an old vent at the east side of the Vatna jokul, called Sveinagja. Previous to this eruption, flames had been seen for no less than eight years issuing from the north side of Vatna, but no lava had flowed down, nor had any ashes been seen ; only slight movements, or earthquakes, had at intervals been noticed both there and farther north.

" The greatest eruption that has taken place was in the beginning of this year, from the " Dyngufjoll," as Mr. Gunnlaugson's map of Iceland called " Aska," situated just in the edge of the great lava field, called " Odatha-hraun." This eruption was very severe at the end of March (1875), and continued from several craters during the whole summer. During the height of this remarkable eruption, volcanic ashes, consisting of triturated pumice stone, were thrown across the north branch of the Atlantic to Norway ; and a considerable quantity on the region leading to Mulu-syssel, damaging many farms in Sudurmulusysln, especially Jokuldalur and Fljvtsdalur. The farms destroyed and damaged were twenty-three in number, of which only four or five were entirely destroyed. On the whole it may be said that the damage done by this eruption has been a little exaggerated in nearly all foreign newspapers, owing to the vivid impression made by the first outbreak, which, to tell the truth, was a very violent one.

" In order fully to comprehend this outbreak, it must be remembered that Iceland is traversed by a broad volcanic belt, running from south to north-north-east, from the Atlantic to the Polar Sea. The principal volcanoes on this line are the innumerable peaks and craters of the great "Vatnajokul," an enormous plateau of ice-covered mountains where fire and frost are continually at war. The greatest damage done to Iceland by volcanic action has arisen from this great centre. On the south flank of the Vatna we have the Skapta jokul, which made the great volcanic eruption of 1783 ; which, according to Lyell, poured out the largest amount of lava that ever flowed from a crater in the historic period. Enormous tracts of land, once the most fertile places in Iceland, have been converted into barren deserts by the volcanic vents of Vatna. We have special names for these sandy deserts, never more to be inhabited by human beings, as " Myrdals sandur," " Solheima sandur," and " Sheydarar sandur."

" Turning to the north side of this same Vatna, you find no less clear marks of the subterranean fire and forces, not only in that enormous lava field called " Odatha-hraun " (the lava of the outlaws or ungodly people), by far the most extensive in Iceland, but also in " Trölladyngur " and the deserts of Myvatn, and the sandy deserts of " Mödurdal," from which some of the latest eruptions of last winter came. Continuing in a north direction, you meet the great solfataras at Myvatn, with the volcanoes Leirhnukur and Krabla ; and from that and the lake of Myvatn is a continuous lava field to Skjalfanda Bay, the northern end of the above mentioned volcanic belt.

" The great Vatna glacier was crossed during this summer by Mr. Watts, an Englishman ; but on account of the bad weather and the difficulties he had to overcome, he could not make many investigations on the glacier itself. He was guided by five young and strong Icelanders, and he confesses that to them he owes his life ; they came near perishing from cold and privation, and, although well fitted out, were much reduced when they came to human dwellings, about fifty English miles from the northern flank of the glacier. Nobody has before crossed this enormous lava field, and few tourists will again try to do it. They went on foot, their horses going round to the east point of the glacier ; they found the thermometer on the glacier to indicate for several days 5° to 2° Fahr.

"Our summer is now over, and the autumn has begun, not unfavorably, but with rather mild weather and southerly winds. Our hay harvest (and this is the only harvest we have), and that of potatoes and turnips, have been favorable ; so we may look forward with some confidence."

According to the latest and reliable accounts, no persons are known to have perished, and no change has taken place in the geysers at Haukadal.

Mica Schist.

Page 277, last line but 4. In a box of specimens sent by Dr. Hjaltalin is one of mica schist. He says : "This I look upon as the basement stone of Iceland, for it is found in many places at the foot of the mountains. The palagonite is not the basement rock of Iceland, for our island no doubt rests immediately upon the so-called 'transition rocks ;' and in proof of this I can offer more indications."

Mineral Springs.

Page 287, last line. "I have during this summer (1875), writes Dr. Hjaltalin, "detected a whole system of carbonated iron springs in a mountain called ' Hengil,' between the lake of Thingvalla and Reykjavik. These springs are of the same nature as the chalybeate springs of Germany, of Reiners, Pyrmont, &c. ; they contain not only bicarbonate of iron, but also of manganese, with other carbonates, and they act remarkably well in several nervous diseases, scrofula, chlorosis, &c. They are found in several other places, especially in the western part of the island, but those recently discovered by me are the most effective. All such springs are in our language called ' Olmeldur.' "

First Legislative Diet.

Page 305, line 25. Dr. Hjaltalin writes : "The duties of our Diet have at this time put such a burden upon me that I have been obliged to devote all my time to them. Now (August, 1875) we have finished, and glad I am, for I was really much exhausted by the daily sittings at the Althing and the never ending committee meetings. We have been obliged to do our work in a great hurry, having no less than eighty-two propositions to consider in the short time of fifty days. Our first legislative Diet was quiet and unanimous, and I should think rather business like, for no less than thirty-seven laws were finished during its short session."

Cambridge: Press of John Wilson & Son.

For EU product safety concerns, contact us at Calle de José Abascal, 56–1°,
28003 Madrid, Spain or eugpsr@cambridge.org.

www.ingramcontent.com/pod-product-compliance
Ingram Content Group UK Ltd.
Pitfield, Milton Keynes, MK11 3LW, UK
UKHW010351140625
459647UK00010B/993